AMAZING GRACE

Amazing Grace

The Nine Principles of Living in Natural Magic

A Galactic Cliff-Hanger

David Wolfe & Nick Good

North Atlantic Books
Berkeley, California

Published by
North Atlantic Books
P.O. Box 12327
Berkeley, California 94712

Cover design by Print.Net, Inc. (www.printnetinc.com)
Cover: Christ Eyes from Christ Risen by Maga (www.magamania.net)
Printed in the United States of America

Amazing Grace is sponsored by the Society for the Study of Native Arts and Sciences, a nonprofit educational corporation whose goals are to develop an educational and cross-cultural perspective linking various scientific, social, and artistic fields; to nurture a holistic view of arts, sciences, humanities, and healing; and to publish and distribute literature on the relationship of mind, body, and nature.

North Atlantic Books' publications are available through most bookstores. For further information, visit our Web site at www.northatlanticbooks.com or call 800-733-3000.

Disclaimer: This book is sold for information purposes only. Neither the authors nor the publisher will be held accountable for the use or misuse of the information contained in this book. This book is not intended as medical or dental advice, because the authors and publisher of this work are not medical doctors and do not recommend the use of mineral-deficient foods, drugs, or medicines to achieve extraordinary health, beauty, spiritual radiance, and to alleviate all health challenges. Because there is always some risk involved, the authors, publisher, and/or distributors of this book are not responsible for any adverse effects or consequences of any kind resulting from the use or misuse of any suggestions or procedures described hereafter.

Library of Congress Cataloging-in-Publication Data
Wolfe, David, 1970–
   Amazing grace : the nine principles of living in natural magic : a galactic cliff-hanger / David Wolfe & Nick Good.
      p. cm.
   Summary: "Stories, quotes, and poems elucidate the authors' presentation of nine principles of success from the Success Ultra Now Personal Optimization Program (SUNPOP) and Huna, the Hawaiian tradition of self-empowerment"—Provided by publisher.
   ISBN-13: 978-1-55643-730-4
   ISBN-10: 1-55643-730-7
   1. Huna. 2. Success—Miscellanea. 3. Self-actualization
(Psychology)—Miscellanea. I. Good, Charles Nicholas. II. Title.
   BF1623.H85W65 2008
   646.7—dc22
                          2008002789

3 4 5 6 7 8 9 10 SHERIDAN 15 14 13 12 11 10

A Note to the Reader

Amazing Grace is a concise living collection of information detailing the most unique, powerful, exciting cutting-edge tools of possibility ... ever.

To maximize the full value of *Amazing Grace*, one is simply required to think for oneself, question assumptions, and smile.

You can read straight through this book from the first page to the last or you can read straight through this book from the last page to the first or you can skip around. This is a magical book and one can open to any page at any time to find exactly the piece of information needed. The reading will surely prove most fruitful when you read this book in the way you most enjoy! We recommend that you take a glass of fresh spring water, place it on this book for 24 hours, and then drink it to help assimilate the information.

Discovering the information in this book can effect a unique transformation and evolution of awareness, attitude, prosperity, and physical health. Reading this book will increase the likelihood of you repeatedly experiencing the best day ever. We recommend that you experiment with and practice the tools and concepts provided in this book. Many viewings of the material and careful review of the content will help to implement new ideas and information into the best lifestyle ever. Do the best you can to open your heart to the incredible majesty of living.

May Amazing Invincible Grace guide your every step.

Many of the products mentioned in this book are available online. We recommend that citizens and superheroes alike enjoy the most incredible and unique health and beauty foods as well as organic products available in the world today. Seek products inspired by principles of sustainable organic agriculture, heart-centered ethics, and living in harmony with nature and the cosmos.

On the title page of this book, we see the logo containing the four circles of physical, mental, emotional, and spiritual vitality. Purity and Love flowing together as a synthesis of wholeness and of balance.

The living expression and embodiment of optimal attitude, awareness, and biology automatically catalyzes a conscious interface with the rainbow cascade of the Holy Spirit—*the whole Spirit*—affecting the biology, affecting the light body, affecting the emotional and mental bodies, and weaving the soul together in an optimal state of being—a state of being known as *Amazing Grace*.

Amazing Grace

Contributing Authors:

David Wolfe, J.D., Superhero, Superfoodist, Orator, Herbalist, Chocolatier, Tree Planter, Alchemist, Cosmic Plumber, Essene Bishop.

Nick Good, D.D. Met. D., Superhero, Superfoodist, Story-Teller, Soulsurfer, Gardener, founder of Success Ultra Now.

Written in Kauai, Hawaii, and in various places throughout the world.

Enjoy the contents of this magical book, a book near and dear to our hearts, and remember to always . . . *Have The Best Day Ever!*

Now you can give this book the strength of ten books.

This copy of *Amazing Grace* originally belonged to:

_____

This book is designed to be passed along to as many people as possible. It is never to be found on a shelf collecting dust. After you have read this book, please pass it along to at least ten others.

This book has been read by:

1. Kathleenie Lane
2. _____
3. _____
4. _____
5. _____
6. _____
7. _____
8. _____
9. _____
10. _____

Acknowledgments

We both wish to thank our mothers for their strength, their optimism, their love.

Dedication

This book is dedicated to all the superheroes of the world: past, present, and future. These women and men of outstanding accomplishment, character, and spiritual beauty are inspirations to us all.

"The answer is never the answer. What's really interesting is the mystery. If you seek the mystery instead of the answer, you'll always be seeking. I've never seen anybody really find the answer—they think they have, so they stop thinking. But the job is to seek mystery, evoke mystery, plant a garden in which strange plants grow and mysteries bloom. The need for mystery is greater than the need for an answer."

—KEN KESEY

"The greater the difficulty the more glory surrounding it. Skillful pilots gain their reputation from storms and tempests."

—EPICTETUS

"Champions aren't made in gyms. Champions are made from something they have deep inside them—a desire, a dream, a vision."

—MUHAMMAD ALI

"Don't ask yourself what the world needs. Ask yourself what makes you come alive, and go do that, because what the world needs is people who have come alive."

—HOWARD THURMAN

"Classical knowledge may be all wrong, such with the perfect Copernican circles, the ellipses of Kepler, the empty space of Einstein, the air-germs of Pasteurian bacteriologists, the atomic nature of the Universe, etc. To see new things from scratch, to expect the impossible to be true, belongs to the emotional equipment of the true pioneering scientist."

—WILHELM REICH

TABLE OF CONTENTS

YOU ARE BEING CALLED

"May you be reborn in exciting times."
—CHINESE PROVERB

This is the moment we have all been waiting for.

You are being called. You have spent your entire existence preparing for this incredible time. Inside, you have always known that you possess something grand, something extraordinary. Upon reflection, the planetary crisis is really a crisis that is motivating you to tap this inner potential of your spirit-soul. The moment draws near. Step into your destiny. It is time to turn yourself on to *Amazing Grace* and *The Nine Principles of Living in Natural Magic*.

Amazing Grace ushers in a whole new type of success—a success that exudes from the soul regardless of outer circumstance. A success established upon an undeniable and irrefutable joyous fact: that an extraordinarily potent natural resource exists within and around us. It is a resource often referred to as God's Love, the Light, the Tao (Dao), the Force, and is known by many other names. The language of quantum physics is calling it The Unified Field of Infinite Possibility. Rumi called it The Friend. Jesus called it The Father. However you label it, the amazing news is that now it is our time to explore, experiment, and discover how to utilize this infinite natural resource to achieve our destiny. *Amazing Grace* and *The Nine Principles of Living in Natural Magic* are designed to assist us in doing just that while at the same time creating a startling shift in consciousness. This shift is a literal activation of the most powerful human possibility. The *superhero archetype* is born.

Amazing Grace asks you to embrace the great glory of living life to the fullest. In the name of honor, wonder, beauty, and all that is sacred, *Amazing Grace* asks you to step forward into the majesty of the greatest flow ever.

You are the heir to all the ages, in the foremost ranks of all time. Every one of your ancestors still lives in you right now. All their aspirations, hopes, and desires are in you. You are the quintessential product of their dreams—which are now your dreams. They prepared you for living as a real-life character in *the greatest love story ever told*.

Stand ready to open your heart, to transform your soul, and to live in natural magic in what is shaping up to be *the great drama of the ages*. Join an ingenious alliance of beings ready, willing, and able to reinvigorate the human soul and save the planet at the last possible second. Take personal responsibility for your destiny and for the destiny of our home—Earth.

This is the best day ever.

Almighty winds of change are sweeping across the toxic plains of an industrial civilization. Tiny flowers, everywhere, are squeezing through the cracks of thick layers of concrete, driven by an unstoppable power. The birds are singing and a message is blowing high in the treetops. The sunrise and sunsets are broadcasting it, and every ocean wave is delivering the same good news. A power now comes alive, without which we cannot escape the darkest predictions that foretell of imminent hell upon Earth. As the old saying goes, it ain't over until it's over. The greatest love story ever is about to be told. *Amazing Grace* informs us that you are to play a starring role.

PSALM 91

He that dwelleth in the secret place of the most High shall abide under the canopy of protection of the Almighty.

I will say of the LORD, He is my refuge and my fortress: my God; in him will I trust.

Surely he shall deliver thee from the snare of the fowler, and from the noisome pestilence.

He shall cover thee with his feathers, and under his wings shalt thou trust: his truth shall be thy shield and buckler.

Thou shalt not be afraid for the terror by night; nor for the arrow that flieth by day;

Nor for the pestilence that walketh in darkness; nor for the destruction that wasteth at noonday.

A thousand shall fall at thy side, and ten thousand at thy right hand; but it shall not come nigh thee.

Only with thine eyes shalt thou behold and see the reward of the wicked.

Because thou hast made the LORD, which is my refuge, even the most High, thy habitation;

There shall no evil befall thee, neither shall any plague come nigh thy dwelling.

For he shall give his angels charge over thee, to keep thee in all thy ways.

They shall bear thee up in their hands, lest thou dash thy foot against a stone.

Thou shalt tread upon the lion and adder: the young lion and the dragon shalt thou trample under foot.

Because he hath set his love upon me, therefore will I deliver him: I will set him on high, because he hath known my name.

He shall call upon me, and I will answer him: I will be with him in trouble; I will deliver him, and honor him.

With long life will I satisfy him, and show him my salvation.

PREFACE

The world today is crying out for superheroes who are willing and able to stand inside the protection of the Almighty. The world today calls for living, whole (holy) embodiments of enlightened blissful health, peace-filled love, and cosmic laughter. The world calls for the disposal of all aspects of the "problem." *Now is the time to embody all aspects of the "solution."*

There are many stories, particularly from the Vietnam War, where men felt they were divinely protected because they read **Psalm 91** every day. Why is this so? As far as we are concerned it is a natural consequence of being in harmony with *that level of Grace* only evoked by the highest levels of *inspiration*.

There is a way of being which manifests as invincibility. There are ways to be incredibly constructive and highly empowered at all times. Each one of us can exceed every expectation and perform at super-hero levels. *Amazing Grace* and *The Nine Principles of Living in Natural Magic* are about choosing a way of being that *embodies* the most constructive, beneficial, and positive thoughts, words, and actions ever. They deliver clues to help us return to a way of love, of innocence, of gratitude, compassion and awe. They are about getting ALL our powers back and then some. They are about making a difference by being the difference. They are about living in natural magic, of being in tune, of walking in Grace. They are about changing the world for the better, together, forever.

This is the greatest love story that has ever been told. It is the story of triumph against all odds, when we finally throw off the shackles of self-imposed slavery and, through the best attitude ever, enlightened awareness, massive action, and an opening of our hearts to the Mystery, we each achieve superhero consciousness and create a life experience for which we are born and for which we yearn. It is a love story that chronicles the saving of the planet from the manifestations of unbalanced, unchecked corrosive energies in all their myriad forms. It is a love story wherein the human soul falls in love again with that

Amazing Invincible Grace with which it is destined to dance and play for all eternity.

Perhaps, best of all, it is a love story in which we *ALL* get to have a starring role.

Yet no love story could be complete without the necessary dynamics of intrigue, mystery, opposition, peril, the rescue, and a harrowing climax. The polar opposition to the lead cast of characters is intrinsic to the key scenes and makes the story come to life.

That opposition in our story consists of a hidden cadre of the world-controlling, politically active, super-rich banking families known as the Illuminati, who rule through deception, massive disinformation, and puppet governments operated by money and destructive energies. This conspiracy may be real or imagined, yet its possibility delivers intrigue and suspense into our story. This "evil" holds hidden a horrific secret agenda of a one-world government with a micro-chipped population of serfs steadily being turned into diseased, unthinking, unfeeling robots run on fear. What is at stake is everything we hold dear—our most unique and natural resources—and these are the immense creativity of our own souls and the resplendent beauty of our beloved planet Earth.

In essence, "good" and "evil" are necessary dynamic opposites that in interaction with each other create either growth or decay. As long as creative forces of "good" bind corrosive forces of "evil," upward evolvement will occur. The role of the superhero is to assist in the identification and the binding of "evil" and to further the creative expression of the human soul and the beautification of the entire planet Earth as we achieve our destiny in the stars—otherwise known as "happily ever after."

That statement aside, any attempt to present the mystery of life in a tidy way with "evil" on this side and "good" on the other is greatly oversimplifying the matter. The only safe and healthy perspective is to *align oneself internally* and appreciate totally *the essence of life*, which empowers the dynamic interaction of opposites. It is only by being truly rooted in this dynamic that one can maintain a sufficiently balanced and aware perspective, a perspective from which it may be safe to consider all the information within *Amazing Grace*.

In general, currently and planetarily, it appears that corrosive forces of "evil" are binding constructive forces of "good." This is a disharmonious, imbalanced surface state of affairs. As human consciousness has developed technologies that use corrosive fuels, the "rusty" nature of destruction has reached an enormous level, threatening the entire planet, and adding a rip current of unprecedented peril to the greatest story ever told.

In spite of all this, the luminous light that guides the unwavering superhero through seemingly impossible odds, opposition, and peril is actually a way of being that gives life extraordinary meaning under *any* circumstances. The superhero habitually tunes in to the essence of the inspiration instigated by reading **Psalm 91.** The superhero understands that the key relationship is always between the Creator and oneself. S/he understands that the establishment of inner harmony and paradise consciousness must *precede* the establishment of outer peace and paradise on Earth. The superhero embodies a way of being that consistently remains in tune and in harmony with cosmic magic, with all that is beautiful and wholesome, with the manifestation of laughter consciousness, with the X-factor—with Amazing Invincible Grace.

ᴐ⁄ᴐ

"Ye are not here to struggle with things, but with gods."
—Jacob Boehme

Introduction

Love, adventure, romance. Magic. Comic relief. Mystery, action, surprise, peril, cosmic drama, and heart-stopping, nail-biting, thrilling suspense. Sound like a good story? Well, it is and guess what? YOU are starring in it. Right now, whether you realize it or not, whether you believe it or not, YOU are starring in the greatest love story that has ever been told.

What you are about to read is a perspective, a point of view, on the current global and, indeed, galactic situation that concerns every single one of us right now. It is a point of view embracing an incredible amount of information distilled into ultra-potent simplicity born from a 45+-year investigation and augmented by the greatest living hearts and minds in world history.

This view includes the following points of interest:

Points of Interest

❖ **The Magical Power of Awareness:** Awareness is primary. Consciousness itself is about awareness. The magical idea states that with increasing awareness comes increasing consciousness that leads to increasing choices, which creates increasing freedom.

❖ **The Secret Power of Attitude:** The perfect attitude is the eternal spring of abundance out of which all success in life ushers forth. The perfect attitude **is** the best attitude ever, one of inspiration, compassion, and forgiveness; it is one that encompasses a loving, heart-enriching state of being; it embraces an attitude of wonder that eternally opens to and explores the mystery. Thomas Jefferson wrote: *Nothing can stop the man with the right mental attitude from achieving his goal; nothing on earth can help the man with the wrong mental attitude.*

❖ You (and every other human being) possess an incredibly creative inner potential, an energy, a life force, full of intelligence, indescribable beauty, and natural magical wonder. It is called your *SOUL.*

We transform the world by activating the full depth and magnitude of our *SOUL POWER*. Soul Power is the most powerful force in the universe that, when aligned wholly with its Great Parent (God), becomes an invincible force of Natural Goodness. Soul power is not something we develop but is actually always present inside our inspiration.

❖ The Truth is always stranger than fiction.

❖ Today is the best day ever. All we have is this day. This time. This moment. The past is gone forever. Tomorrow will never arrive. The best day ever must occur today.

❖ Synchronicities are major divine clues that you are on the correct path.

❖ Everything in moderation—especially moderation.

❖ The ability to learn and *master* anything *immediately* may very well become the most important skill of the future. The technology of superhuman potential is here now. To access it all and actually use it we must first *believe* that we can master anything immediately.

❖ The best approach to anything in life is a "minimum optimum" approach that allows each individual or group to continuously discover ways of doing more with less. This is the ultimate goal of every technology.

❖ **Raw Logic:** The mere idea that every single ghost experience, Bigfoot sighting, UFO encounter, alien abduction, psychic occurrence of any kind, Loch Ness monster viewing, conspiracy theory, etc., is the product of a neurosis or hallucination is patently and completely ridiculous. The burden of proof is clearly on the doubter. The doubter must prove that every single paranormal experience out of thousands or even millions of such encounters in each category is a phony. That is impossible. If even one UFO encounter is real, then they exist. If even one Bigfoot sighting or footprint is real, then they exist. If even one alien abduction experience is real, then people are actually being abducted by aliens. If even one ghost story is true, then ghosts exist. If even one person can see into the future, then seeing into the future is possible. This is Raw Logic and it instantly deconstructs and eliminates any fog of confusion surrounding paranormal phenomena. The overall depth of the mystery of life is as great as ever.

❖ **The Best News Ever:** God has been found in everything. Every atom, every cell, every life form, every human, every planet, every star, and every galaxy contains a singularity (a black hole, wormhole, or sacred heart) with an event horizon (e.g. electron field, cell membrane, skin, atmosphere, solar wind, etc.). *Each singularity is a sacred heart that is directly connected to God.* As nuclear physicist Nassim Harramein (www.theresourceproject.org) has discovered and mathematically proven, energy and information emerge from and are drawn into a double toroid shape (a double toroid is two donut-like objects sitting one on top of the other) that surrounds each singularity. This energy and information flow and interact with internal information as well as with information at and beyond the event horizon, and then this energy and information feed the updated "news" back into the sacred heart singularity (God). Basically, all energies go out from their home, experience the world, and come back home with the news.

❖ "You are what you eat" is the "zip" file we downloaded from our Creator when we were e-mailed to the planet at birth. This axiom reflects an inescapable habit of each object in the quantum field— to attract to itself those things that are in harmony with its own nature—yet each object's own nature is always being modified by choices. In simple terms, "you are what you eat" is an inescapable fact of quantum reality. Eat the best food ever, and observe the results over time. Eat the worst food ever, and observe the results over time. Compare and contrast.

❖ **Raw Food is Medicine:** Eating and growing mineral-rich, love-rich, living, raw plant food ennobles consciousness and accelerates optimal biological health transformation. We suggest that you experiment with raw-food nutrition, play with it, love it, enjoy it.

Have great fun with what you eat, and get all those great foods going through you more and more and more. For raw assistance, please read our books: *The Sunfood Diet Success System, Eating For Beauty,* and *Naked Chocolate.*

❖ The less you eat, the longer you live, so the more you get to eat.

❖ **Unconditional Laughter.** This may be the highest vibration in the universe. The best story ever is interspersed with the most clever comic relief ever.

❖ Growth and decay are the result of a particular dynamic interaction of opposites. As long as constructive "good" interacts and binds with corrosive "evil," growth will predominate. When corrosive "evil" interacts and binds with constructive "good," decay will predominate. The forces in nature are never in balance—the yin-yang symbol is incorrect—overall constructive forces must predominate in the universe or nothing could exist. Interestingly, it appears that corrosive forces predominate momentarily when wise nature is clearing the path for a new evolution. Corrosive forces inevitably burn up their fuel (fuel originally created by constructive energies) and by natural law, constructive forces (which are fueled by free energy—life itself) begin to rebind corrosive forces.

❖ **Judgment and Denial: the source of disharmony?** Both denying dualism and judging dualism are out of accordance with the natural rhythm of life, which consists of an eternal, dynamic interaction of opposites. Dualism is intrinsic to all manifestations of life.

❖ Any and every physiological symptom from a toothache to terminal cancer has its roots in thoughts, words, and actions. Any and every physiological symptom from joy to unconditional laughter has its roots in thoughts, words, and actions. You are who you are and what you are as a result of the sum total of your thoughts, words, and actions and consequential feeling states.

❖ **Dharma:** What is required in the world today is the total, complete, and focused activation of your mission. It is when we are set alight with the vision of our true purpose and we are on the mission that life wants us to fulfill that we become truly happy and therefore healthy. A soul living in tune with its internal purpose is bound to create utter magic. The purpose of the seed is to become the mighty tree and to continuously bear fruit and spread seeds.

❖ It is going to take *everything* you have got to become all that you can be.

❖ **Spirituality and Technology are intimately intertwined.** Technology is actually the most spiritual phenomenon going on in our collective reality (dimension). What creates heaven or hell? Technology. What is directing the fate of this reality? The fate of our Earth? Technology. This is exactly what we are not being told. Ever. It is never mentioned at all. Yet it is the most obvious thing. Look around—pollution, famine, greed, all of these karmic imprints are directly related to the technology of our day, a technology of weapons that arms the state against the common person, a technology of manipulation that informs the common person with lies, a technology of machines that runs on corrosive thermodynamic energies (e.g. wood, coal, oil, nuclear). We could have a constructive technology based on water and air machines that run entirely on cooling formative energies (which is the same free energy that every life-form taps into). Free energy machines will be created spontaneously when enough of our collective consciousness allows for it. The solution to the world's problems is, in large part, technological.

❖ The way some individuals have been living their lives, feeding their biology and orienting their attitudes, values, beliefs, and awarenesses, *has created* extraordinary synchronicity, prosperity, joy, magic, harmony, laughter, love, health, and grace.

❖ The way some individuals have been living their lives, feeding their biology and orienting their attitudes, values, beliefs, and awarenesses, *has created* extraordinary disease, destruction, hate, famine, war, anger, frustration, doubt, pessimism, despair, and materialism.

❖ **We are all being influenced by highly benevolent hidden spiritual forces.** A pre-ordained, very well organized strategy is being played out by Gaia (the spirit of the Earth itself), by devas, gnomes, fairies, sylphs, nymphs, sprites, spirits, angels, celestial intelligences, aliens, shamans, eco-yogis, activated light-workers, environmental activists as well as by a collection of planetary superheroes to the benefit of the human family, the total beautification of the physical environment, and the ennobling of galactic consciousness.

❖ We are all being influenced by highly malevolent, covert, political, and intriguing forces—a group we refer to as the Illuminati (whether the Illuminati exist as a formal cabal/conspiracy or not, they certainly exist as an archetype of consciousness in opposition). As the story unfolds, the Illuminati are enacting a pre-planned, very well organized agenda that is being played out by the owners of the banking-military-pharmaceutical-petrochemical-agribusiness-industrial complex to the detriment of the human family and our Mother Earth. The complexities of a regime that bombards and obliterates Mother Nature and our inner nature with so much calculated destruction are now understood and exposed. The antidote to "evil" is inside us all and is the superhero's magic potion. When fully imbibed, ordinariness is superceded by extra-ordinariness, and the perceiver of the problem becomes the embodiment of the solution.

❖ The battle for possession of the human soul between the dynamic archetypal forces of "good" and "evil" is raging in the *matrix* we call our world. This supplies the drama, the dynamic interplay of opposites, the precarious peril that makes the greatest love story ever told come to life in stunning vividness. The story is definitely a bit more exciting if the superhero must save the love of their life from an "evil" arch-nemesis.

❖ A direct consequence of completely aligning our consciousness with the constructive forces of growth and levity is the activation of heretofore hidden superpowers of incredible potential, love, beauty, technological insight, and harmony. Soon a "Heaven on Earth" reality comes into view.

❖ The direct consequences of a constriction and the corrosive distortion of pure individual soul-power energy flow are disease and all forms of disharmony. In the *matrix,* part of our reality has been engineered by a manipulation of our worst fears. The clearest way to save the planet from psychic and ecological catastrophe is for *everyone* to do the best s/he can to turn unconditionally towards *LOVE,* heart-centered thoughts, words, and deeds. This means, "stop working for Big Brother and start working for the Mother." "Quit your job" and become a superhero.

❖ The greatest love story that's ever been told is the story of each human being awakening to her/his soul power (often with her/his soulmate-partner) in a plot of dynamic intrigue, receiving their passport to the cosmos and consciously choosing to create "Heaven on Earth" via thought, word, and deed as true superheroes prepared to do what it takes to achieve an extraordinary, divinely assisted destiny.

❖ The current time in human history is the most exciting era ever to be alive. It is a time of unlimited and extreme possibility. New realities are literally being defined by the way we express our soul power in the eternal flow of time—moment to moment.

❖ Approaching day-to-day life as a mystery with clues presented synchronistically—clues that, when acted upon and followed through to their appropriate conclusion, lead the detective to more and more unique awarenesses, experiences of consciousness, love, laughter, wonder, and hope—appears to be very close to the intent of the Universal Soul (God). Life can unfold in the most fascinating way ever when we become aware *that life has always been a mystery novel with clues that have been consistently provided all along.* Mysteries, anomalies, paradoxes, clues, cleverly developed solutions, and surprise endings are archetypically interwoven into the greatest love story ever told.

❖ Our secret inner nature is now and has always been peaceful, loving, wise, intelligent, forgiving, wonder-filled, grateful, and kind.

❖ Because of a legacy of poor, ingrained habits, recorded-distorted emotional attitudes (unresolved karma) and mental conditioning, we commit ourselves as superheroes to: *practice on a consistent DAILY basis the attitudes, habits, and awarenesses that will allow our soul power to fully express originally and creatively.*

❖ Everything we require to manifest our highest destiny is already here right around us now.

❖ The way you do anything is the way you do everything.

❖ The world changes once we change.

☯

"Salvation of the world depends on me."
—*A Course in Miracles*, Lesson 186

Raw Magic
The Nine Principles of Living In Natural Magic

Principle Number One: Grace

This is the story of John Newton, a sea captain who was intimately involved in a remarkable incident that occurred in the year 1748.[1] Back in that time the ships had big galleys, made of wood, all hand crafted. Each ship was like a work of art, with all the sails, and ropes were made of hemp. These sailing ships were not only true works of art, but free-energy machines that were powered by the gifts of the wind.

When traveling across the vast oceans in those days, powered by large square-rigged sails, dependent on wind and weather, a captain couldn't really know what was going to happen on those journeys, but rather had to be guided by feeling.

Captain Newton used to sail from London, heading south down the coastlines of the Old World to pick up his cargo, and then would turn to sail to the New World across the ocean. It was during one particular journey, about halfway across the Atlantic, that he noticed the swells starting to increase, causing the ship to rock and sway unusually. Captain Newton began to sense trouble ahead.

The swells started getting bigger, and then the ocean became choppy. The wind picked up. And Captain Newton realized that perhaps he was a little late in the season for an Atlantic crossing, and that there could be a major storm ahead. The conditions continued to get worse, and worse, and worse.

Now back in those days, the ship's wheel—the steering column of the vessel—had to be held at all times, because if let go, the rudder would turn completely left or right, causing a ship to spin one way or the other, and to start going in a circle. So there had to be a man on deck to stand at the ship's wheel at all times, no matter what the weather or what the situation, and that was usually the captain. And so this is where Captain John Newton found himself that day, on the deck, as the storm began to set in, holding onto the wheel of his ship.

As conditions continued to worsen, he had his men climb up the ship's tall masts and pull down all the sails. Now, in that kind of a situation, as the waves start to increase in height and occasionally spill over the top of the ship, it was common for crew members to be sent down below and tie themselves to parts of the ship, because if the ship were to come apart in the storm, at least each man would have something to hold onto in that ocean.

An interesting thing in this case, a thing we have purposely kept hidden until this point, was the cargo of John Newton's ship. Below the deck one would not find wine, olive oil, or textiles. Below the deck were over a hundred people chained to the floor. A living, breathing cargo. Captain John Newton was a slave captain, in the business of transporting slaves. Based in England, he would sail from London, stop in Spain for supplies, then travel all the way down to present-day Ghana (Africa), where he would pick up his cargo. He would cross the Atlantic to North America to drop off his human cargo, and then sail back across the ocean to London, in a protracted triangular route.

Below the deck, these people were bound in chains to the floor of the ship. They could hardly move or do anything at all, and now they were subject to the rising swells and resulting sea sickness, which soon turned into ten-foot and even occasional twenty-foot waves crashing over the sides of the ship and spilling huge quantities of icy-cold sea-water on top of these Africans.

And on this trip, this galley of human cargo was in a lot of trouble. After pulling all the sails down, Captain Newton sent all his men down below. Large quantities of water were by then spilling into the ship, and the Captain feared absolute and final calamity: the ship breaking up. It was all he could do to actually hold onto the ship's wheel, and so he had his second-in-command come up and chain him to it, because if the ship began spinning it would be doomed by the onslaught of swells.

The storm became torrential; it rained so hard that Captain Newton could hardly even see what was in front of him, let alone direct the ship perpendicular into the swells to avoid a deadly, parallel slap by one or more twenty-foot waves, which would quickly bust the ship's frame apart.

And interestingly enough, these people down below who were chained to the floor of the ship, and who could see nothing of what was going on, jarred and jerked on the ocean with torrents of ice-cold salt water dumped on them every few minutes, these people—instead of screaming, crying, yelling, wailing, demanding—began to sing together what sounded like a hymn or a prayer. And that prayer came from the "Ah-Om" languages, originating all the way back in Ancient Egypt. The song had no lyrics, just tones.

They sang so loud that Captain Newton heard the ancient hymn, even over the roaring sound of that wind and rain in what was clearly deteriorating into hurricane conditions. Over and over they delivered it like a mantra, an affirmation, while the conditions on that deck became so intense that John Newton, as he stood lashed to the wheel of the ship, began to sing too. Just to keep his sanity, he began to make up lyrics that he created that very moment, fitting them to the song he heard coming up from the enslaved people below.

At the climax of that whole evening, when the rain was so torrential and he so exhausted that he could barely stand and hold on to the ship, chained to the wheel, he was only able to continue on because of the power of the souls of the people down below. They continued to sing in spite of their captivity, their distance from home, and their being on the brink of death. At that moment, Captain John Newton swore that if he made it—if they all made it—he would let them all go, return his shipping licenses, and become a minister.

Captain John Newton made it through that dark night of the soul. Everyone on that ship weathered that death-defying experience; they survived the storm. The sails were put back up and, as the story goes, they turned the ship around, set sail back to Africa, and John New-ton let everybody go. Then Newton sailed back to London, turned in his shipping licenses, became a minister, and wrote down the lyrics of the still-present and well-tuned song that guided him through that stormy night, which he began to preach in his church. The song is called *Amazing Grace.* It's an ancient African prayer with English lyrics.

Amazing Grace!
(How sweet the sound)
That saved a wretch like me!
I once was lost, but now am found,
Was blind, but now I see.

'Twas grace that taught my heart to fear,
And grace my fears relieved;
How precious did that grace appear,
The hour I first believed!

Thru' many dangers, toils, and snares,
I have already come;
'Tis grace has brought me safe thus far,
And grace will lead me home.

The Lord has promised good to me,
His word my hope secures;
He will my shield and portion be,
As long as life endures.

Yes, when this flesh and heart shall fail,
And mortal life shall cease;
I shall possess, within the veil,
A life of joy and peace.

The earth shall soon dissolve like snow,
The sun forbear to shine;
But God, who called me here below,
Will be forever mine.

Captain John Newton's story flows down through the ages due to its power to touch our soul, the very core of our humanness. The story touches archetypal soul powers of inspiration based on courage, will, song, compassion, and joining together as one human family. It lights the path and guides us through all the pages of this book. It continually informs us that no matter what situation we face, there is a way out, there is an X-factor that can be invoked through the power of Grace.

The time-tested ancient phrase states: "It ain't over until it's over."

When we're shackled underneath that ship, *all options are not lost.* As long as we live and breathe, we can become aware that we always have a choice. As ice-cold ocean water is dumped on us, we can whine and complain and point fingers or we can turn towards grace, love, beauty, and the power of our souls. Interestingly enough, through the influence of the heart (channeled in communication through song) we are also able to direct soul power to our ship's captain, who is totally and previously unconscious of his crimes. And through that heart-felt communication, an *Amazing Grace* can give him the strength to make it through the night, transform his being, turn the ship around, and save instead of destroy lives.

This story is extremely deep and metaphorical. When the choice was before those people, they could have responded with any emotion: rage, despair, terror. But what they chose was love, beauty, and dignity in the form of a song-prayer directly from the heart. A song-prayer so monumental that it saved all of them, and still touches us even today.

Will we allow our soul to sing its song?

"Every human being alive today, modern or tribal, primal or over-domesticated, has a soul that is original, natural and above all, indigenous in one way or another. Like all indigenous peoples today, that indigenous soul of the modern person has either been banished to some far reaches of the dream world or is under direct attack by the modern mind.... For there to be a world at all, every

indigenous, natural thing must start singing its song, dancing its dance, moving and breathing according to its own nature, saying its name, manifesting simultaneously its secret spiritual signature."
—Martín Prechtel, *Secrets of the Talking Jaguar*

ᴏ/ᴏ

The Captain of our ship, according to at least one perspective, is the modern ego-mind, and that ego is currently sailing us into big trouble. We are faced with a choice. And we do have to choose because even not choosing is a choice. At any moment we can choose to align with our destiny, our mission, to allow the song of our soul to come forth and create miracles. The story shows us that. From barbarism to benevolence, from cruelty to kindness, from ignorance to Grace, from murderer to minister. And this is the choice we have to make, because *every one of us,* right now, is on a vessel, in a storm, lashed to the wheel.

What we call upon today is *Amazing Grace* because it has come to that point. What is going on today is so intense on every front—politically, ecologically, physically, and psychically—with the assault on the Earth through nuclear power plants, the chemtrails in the sky, the wars, the political irresponsibility, usury (charging interest on money), and corporate greed that it leads us to continuously ask the key question: What are we going to do about this?

We can always select the miracle of the heart. Even in spite of all that's going on, the situation is not nearly as intense as being an unwilling passenger on that ship in 1748, seasick, chained to the floor in a torrential storm, not having eaten for a week, not being able to look outside, and barely able to see each other. As our friend Riley Martin says, we are all of royal blood and can, at any time, decide that we are going to go back to that level of majesty—that noble level of Grace. It takes practice, but the archetypal movement from brutal slave trader to minister of love is the challenge we are being asked to face.

ᴏ/ᴏ

SOUL POWER

Our history is truly a story of all the souls in this quadrant of the universe. This is the shamanic perspective on it all.

The story of the human soul had, primarily, *until this time*, been a conflict between the natural will of the soul (the pre-ordained calling, career, mission, dharma) and the potential mis-actions of the ego-mind (imposed rules, conformity, false identities). This past conflict had been intimately connected to the cause and root of all disease, all neuroses, all dysfunction. In many cases, the ego-mind had been hijacked and unknowingly programmed, and had functioned in a disharmonious way much of the time—unconsciously.

Now, thanks to the great opening in the technology of human potential, and the simultaneous overall peril of the individual and planetary situation, individuals are dropping the old programs, opening their heart, activating their mission, and using their ego-mind as a tool directed by their heart, instead of the other way around. A new human is emerging—the *superhero*.

The superhero is driven by one single, all-unifying energy—the propulsion of *who they really are*. Superheroes feel their position in the eternal garden, as their souls are planted, seed-like, in God's eternal soil of inspiration. Rooted in a true sense of self, grounded in the fertile earth of compassionate, breath-filled love and wonder, the superhero stretches out shoots and leaves from its trunk and branches and, honorably, courageously, in an enlightened, empowered way guided by Grace, links roots with other soul-centered beings and offers flowers and fruits of thoughts, words, and actions to the cosmos.

You are about to learn, if you didn't already know, that the quintessential battle between the archetypal forces of "good" and "evil" for possession of soul power is taking place against a backdrop of jaw-dropping infinite cosmic magnitude. The fences around the arena within which we had hitherto defined ourselves have been dissolved. The latest round of revelations regarding our position in the cosmos relative to other worlds and their inhabitants has delivered undeniable evidence that utterly redefines the playing fields of life. It is no longer about competing aggressively and selfishly in a material world merely to survive; that awareness program and the attitudes that go with it are obsolete.

Now the power of the Almighty calls for the activation of the superhero who completely aligns with their individual soul mission, unleashing an explosion of soul power into the cosmos—an explosion fueled by love, laughter, forgiveness, compassion, gratitude, wonder and innocent perception, grounded in kindness, the most powerful alchemical blend in the universe.

The energy that we call soul power is the ur-cause of all creativity, of all life, all imagination. More seminal than atomic energy, more propulsive than any rocket, it is the power that properly re-plants the great forests, cleans up the oceans, develops and implements quality-enhancing free-energy technologies, builds the bridges across the eons, travels the cosmos, and elects to be a galactic citizen who lives in awe. *Once we align the will of our soul with our actions, we begin to immediately live in natural magic; we more and more embody the effervescent state of Amazing Grace.*

Every single one of us has her/his own secret spiritual signature, and the shamans say that this is the era in time for every one of us to start *singing that song,* expressing her/his unique mission. So it is the time to listen within and remember our song, to remember who we are.

Somewhere inside you, you know who you are. You are a noble cosmic being, filled to overflowing with unlimited potential, creativity, joy, and capabilities equal to every miracle past, present, and future.

This is the time for action. Now is the best time ever. It looks like reality is heading to heaven and hell at an alarming rate, concurrently. We observe both a continuing gradual decline of consciousness into death's sleep *and simultaneously* an invitation to play our part in the greatest love story that's ever been told. Remember that the choice is ours, every moment, to align consciously with the forces of natural goodness which are lifting the heavy weight of ignorance from humanity's aching back.

∾⊘⊘

Through action—acts of love, kindness and forgiveness, through attitudes of compassion and innocence, by opening to the mystery, by sailing under the wing of Amazing Grace—you are becoming your very own soul-powered superhero. This is something to be realized constantly, all the time, again and again forever.

AMEN.

THE X-FACTOR

Collectively we hold a vision of paradise on Earth. We perceive that the way to get there, the actual strategy at this moment in time, is based on nothing less than a miracle.

We know that there's one wild card that's always available any time, and it is the phenomenon of spontaneous healing, the X-factor. The Earth can be spontaneously healed, just like a person can. People have been, and continue to be, spontaneously healed; it happens every day of the week, all year long, all over the world. We hold the feeling of spontaneous healing close to our hearts and, through that awareness, we move away from more mind-dominated aspirations and open our beings to the miracle, to the *Grace* of God, to the X-Factor.

No one knows what is going to happen to our spinning planet. No one knows what our ultimate fate will be. No one knows if we are going to make it or not. In the midst of a world in chaos and utter transformation we align with the unknown, the impossible, the improbable. From here we will see how the story is to unfold. It's going to be a big surprise—it always is.

THE BEST WORLD EVER

Have you ever written down a goal, and then suddenly it happened? But it happened in a completely different way than you could have predicted?

We practice the idea that every day is the best day ever. After a few of those "best ever" days in a row, you cannot invent how it could get better—you couldn't know. But the Creator knows how it could get better and categorically delivers that to you all the time. This phenomenon occurs outside mind-dominated consciousness. It can only be appreciated in the heart.

The whole idea here is the "best ever"—the use of those words specifically. Why are those words important? Because your mind cannot quite wrap itself around a continuing series of best days ever. Your mind cannot figure out a way *how* it could get better. An assumption is built into the language that automatically turns the result over to the Creator to deliver in miraculous fashion.

So what these two authors are really after, and what we invite you to be a part of, is actually a complete picture of paradise on Earth, a miracle. Our goal is to create, through the Grace of God, the best world ever.

Alien Awareness

"There are more things in heaven and earth, Horatio, than are dreamed of in all your philosophy."
—William Shakespeare

"We shall no longer hang on to the tails of public opinion or to non-existent authority on matters utterly unknown and strange. We shall gradually become experts ourselves in the mastery of the knowledge of the future."
—Wilhelm Reich

It appears, based on all the evidence, that we are not the only tenants in the building. The concept of human solitude in the universe is a well-crafted neurosis—the destructive results of which are self-evident. Consciousness of every sort and variety seems to be doing all it can to occupy every peak and valley of reality. The situation on planet Earth and at all levels of perception has always been and will continue to be "standing room only."

As a point of reference, our friend Riley Martin has been a leading figure in the realm of extraterrestrial phenomena since 1953. His revelations concerning intelligent beings from outside our planetary sphere are deeply relevant to the current planetary situation. Riley's direct contacts with foreign spacecraft are worth your review.

If you are an individual who is immersed in isolation consciousness, we recommend that you suspend judgment until you can *feel* that contact with greater intelligences than ours is at least a remote possibility. Then at that point, read on ...

Awareness is the key. The Grace that we sail under the wing of is much deeper and broader than we could believe. In fact, we can only understand the implications of it at the fringes of our imagination. God's universe is greater, by far, than any human illusion ever taught anywhere.

The alien presence is real, and it masks itself by the most ingenious method possible—incredulity using the absurd. The presence or injection of an absurd component into nearly every UFO or ET experience is exactly *how* the alien presence is able to conceal itself. For example, using UFO ship forms that appear to our eye as a cheap 1950s B-movie spaceship causes any pictures of such a ship to be laughed off as a hoax. Or another example: using sounds for their alien ships that are identical to spaceship sounds in Hollywood movies causes a cognitive confusion (is this real or imagined?) in the consciousness of nearly every person hearing such sounds. And then we have to contend with alien abductions where people experience rectal probes. Such examples of absurd facets to the UFO and ET phenomenon abound. The inability of common consciousness to identify the level of sophistication of the alien presence and its capability of disarming our rational mind, using the absurd, is the key barrier at hand.

Not only are the aliens extremely deceptive and clever at avoiding detection, the Illuminati's alien cover-up is the most elaborate and pervasive of any lie ever told. Yet, in spite of absurd UFO and ET stories and the deliberate monumental attempt to cover up the alien presence, most people actually do still believe in the presence of aliens. They know that UFOs are real and that strange things have been traversing through our atmosphere and our consciousness for a long, long time—probably forever.

Because the extraterrestrial implications are extremely vast and affect every part of our spiritual life as well as our origins and destiny, any discussion of ultimate success and spiritual transformation must rationally acknowledge and explore at least the possibility of an alien presence.

Certainly even modern science is unanimous in its verdict: *it is a mathematical certainty for life to exist on other worlds.*

"There is coming a day very soon when great knowledge will be brought to this plane by wonderful entities who are your beloved brothers. In that time scientific developments will bloom here greater than they ever have. What is coming forth is called The Age of God."

—RAMTHA

As more and more research and details of UFO and ET experiences become available, thanks largely to the Internet, a sobering picture emerges that transcends the boundaries of science fiction and absolutely blows the doors off conventional perspectives. Truth, indeed, is far stranger than fiction. Anyone genuinely interested in downloading the most enlightened and professionally investigated perspectives on the subject should investigate the complete works of Dr. John Mack and Dr. Steven Greer[2] and tune in immediately to www.fastwalkers.com and check out the Google video of the same name.

Dr. John E. Mack (October 4, 1929–September 27, 2004) was a Pulitzer Prize-winning American psychiatrist and professor at Harvard Medical School who, relatively late in his career, became intensely focused on the "alien abduction" phenomenon. Dr. Mack initially suspected that "abductees" were suffering from mental illness, but when no obvious pathologies could be detected in the individuals he was studying, he delved deeper into the subject matter, eventually concluding that the phenomenon was in some way "real." He wrote: "Looking back at the path that brought me to my present viewpoint, I realize that one cannot begin to consider seriously something so preposterous without at least a minimal willingness to look at the possibility that our view of the universe and ways of knowing about it have indeed been incomplete and perhaps flawed." Dr. Mack studied approximately two hundred men and women who reported recurrent alien-encounter experiences. Dr. Mack remains to this day the most esteemed academic to have studied the subject. His research and conclusions are included in two of his books: *Abduction* and *Passport to the Cosmos,* the latter containing fascinating philosophical insights into the nature of the alien presence.

Dr. Steven Greer, author of *Hidden Truth—Forbidden Knowledge,* is at the forefront of research into this amazing arena of interface between humans and extraterrestrial beings. The combination of his personal experience, integrity, and street savvy born from surviving an alcoholic father, emergency room medicine, and radionic murder attempts on his life has sculpted Dr. Greer into quite a powerful ally for good on the planet. His years of research rubbing shoulders with individuals with access to above-top-secret realms of government and Illuminati operations qualify him to speak and write on the subject. Dr. Greer is blessed with not only credentials and credibility, he is also grounded in his approach. Through his Center for the Study of Extraterrestrial Intelligence (CSETI) organization, Dr. Greer has been instrumental in helping to bring individuals "out of the closet," insiders who were involved in various aspects of the alien cover-up. These individuals, with Greer's assistance, have been empowered to appear and speak together and go onto the Congressional record in order to speak officially without fear of reprisals by secret agents within the Illuminati matrix.

Dr. Greer informs us that the majority of the information reaching us on all ET phenomena, including virtually all abduction reports, is being manipulated through a lens of the darkest and most twisted political intrigue ever. His conclusions emphasize that in fact our brothers and sisters from the stars are here to observe, study, and ultimately assist us; and that a massive and focused disinformation policy is being forced upon us via Illuminati-controlled media to convince us otherwise. The extent of the disinformation campaign almost beggars belief as Dr. Greer chronicles the astonishing details of the reverse engineering of "shot-down" ET technology and the application of that technology for horrendous purposes. According to Greer, some "alien abduction" cases are perpetrated by sinister shadow Illuminati agents who have, at this point in time, their own reverse-engineered ET technology and have even engineered their own android-clones which look like the so-called Grey aliens. Many of the cattle mutilations and other seemingly malevolent phenomena are for the specific purposes of seeding fear into the mind of mass consciousness for no other reason than the eventual goal of taking war technology into space to be pointed back upon the Earth at Earth's citizens under the pretext of protecting us from what will eventually be an admitted alien presence and potential threat. The Illuminati may also be arming up space to continuously attack observational alien craft, so more reverse engineering can be done. And, finally, the militarization of space allows the Illuminati to begin to protect their rulership (as the Earth's masters) from alien races who potentially might want to help free us (Earth's citizens).

Whatever the case, the main point to digest is that our biggest threat is not "martians" or "pleaideans" but emotionally distorted humans—ourselves. If we do create our reality, then why not choose to align our powerful creative beliefs with the best ET story ever imaginable? Why choose to believe in blood-sucking reptiles when we can believe in beautiful babes from Sirius, for example? Or stunning Prince Charmings from Alpha Centauri. As always, there are positive and negative sides to all phenomena. Yet, remember, if the aliens were here to destroy us or conquer, they would have done it long ago.

⊘⊘

Consider the Following Safeguard

"Those civilizations which are equal or behind yours cannot reach you any more than you can reach them. There is enough distance between each one to ensure that this will remain true. Those which can draw near have the consciousness to compress great distances. Aside from possible desperation or degeneration, it is not within their consciousness to exploit or to conquer mankind. . . . I would be misleading you to imply that the galactic community is without its points of turbulence and misbehavior, for there is always free will. However, there is a rule that is generally true, and you can rely upon it to give you comfort. Those who could harm you cannot reach you. Those who can reach you would not likely harm you. In His great wisdom, The Creator saw fit to space all life-bearing planets far enough apart to establish this condition. This is combined with a secondary fact that all truly advanced technologies are based on principles of synchronicity, holistic patterning, and respect for the dynamics of life. The idea of marauders traveling at the speed of light and beyond, simply for conquest, is pure fiction. The synchronicity required for that technology simply could not be derived from a consciousness based on conflict."

—Jesus in Glenda Green's book *Love Without End*

The Coming of Tan

We have been fortunate to review the alien presence by the close contact we share with our friend Riley Martin, whose lifetime of continuous and unique interactions with a particular race of aliens is unparalleled.

What we especially appreciate about Riley is his absence of interpretations based on fear. And since fear pervades the entire spectrum of abduction phenomena, alien visitation, mass media, government cover-ups, etc., we can only assume that those fear-generated perspectives distort the truth about the phenomenon.

Riley has been psychically connected to a humanoid alien space-captain named Tan *(O-Qua-Tangin-Wann)* since he was first abducted in rural Arkansas in 1953 at seven years old. Every eleven years, Riley has been revisited by Tan and taken aboard the Great Biaviian Mothership, which at present is in orbit around Saturn. When questioned about how often he is in touch with Tan psychically, he replied, "Two or three times a month."

Riley's story is all online at www.rileymartin.org and may also be found in his audio-book *The Coming of Tan*.

This may sound ridiculous to the uninitiated, but NASA has taken photographs of the Mothership[3] with the recent *Cassini* spacecraft, which is, at this moment, also in orbit around Saturn. *Cassini* has been transmitting images of an unexplained forty-kilometer-wide object that is glowing like a radiating egg just behind Titan, one of Saturn's moons. This object is exactly where Riley Martin has placed the Biaviian Mothership. In fact, he's been telling people the ship is there for decades. (Check out the following link: www.thecomingoftan.com/illuminated_object/illuminated_object.html)

According to Riley, that Mothership has been in orbit in our solar system for eons and, contrary to conspiracy theorists and Illuminati spin-doctors, the visitors on board that ship are simply observing and conducting experiments on the Earth, the Earth's life-forms, and … us.

Quantum physics informs us that there is, of course, an intrinsic problem with all experiments because it is never truly possible to remain only an observer because the observer affects the observed. Therefore, even a simple observational alien presence would affect us at every level of our consciousness, whether we know it or not. But to say that the aliens are only making conventional observations and conducting linear experiments is to oversimplify the situation (although for the most part we believe this is true). The aliens have been getting a little more involved with human affairs than is prudent.

The Biaviian Mothership has actually been an observation and research station for many races of aliens exploring and studying our solar system. The main alien race on the Mothership belongs to Riley's group, the Biaviians, and, as far as is known, they are running the show.

Consider the situation: Tan's race, the Biaviians, ascended (became enlightened) as an entire race and, instead of retreating like good alien yogis into high mountain caves on their planet to meditate on the Light, they decided to build spaceships of extraordinary beauty and technology and sail bravely into the cosmos to explore exactly how great the Light (God) is.

Riley has been telling everybody for his entire life that the Biaviians are here to help. They are our angels, our brothers, our friends—and our genetic relatives. Somehow, in some way, we share genes with our cosmic cousins. In fact, when we search our feelings, everyone knows somewhere deep inside that we are part simian, part alien—part ape, part angel.

Somewhere in our past a race of aliens genetically altered us. We side with Riley and believe that their intent was positive, although beyond the scope of their consciousness; thus over time the experiment went out of control due to human tampering with dangerous interdimensional sorcery (symbolism, ritual, ceremony, sacrifice, etc.). Others, like Michael Tsarion (www.michaeltsarion.com), believe that the original alien intent was negative, and this coupled with sorcery is why the experiment went out of control.

Any way you frame it, the Illuminati have a plan to turn the inevitable universal discovery of the alien presence into yet another scam to gain more control and surveillance. Be aware. Their agenda is to weaponize outer space with so-called "Star Wars" technology by convincing us this is necessary due to an eventual staged, phony alien attack.

By cross-referencing Riley Martin's, Dr. Stephen Greer's, and Dr. John Mack's experiences, testimonies, and reports across a wide range of other books, magazines, videos, and Internet resources, we feel we can safely conclude that the aliens (cosmic angels) are extremely connected to the ancient devic energies of the Earth (Gaia) and to sensible, evolving, consciousness-expanding, Earth-friendly souls described by Tan as "children of the living waters, possessors of the staff of reason." Based on the calculated, greed-directed, technological mis-turns over the last two hundred years and the controlling menace of false masters (the Illuminati), the grand old-growth forests are almost all cut down, the pristine holy rivers are polluted, the skies are filled with cooking soot, depleted uranium weapons are being used without a second thought, and the ancient planetary devas that have filled the planet's ecosystems for millions of years with their magic are retreating due to the destruction. The great Earth is in peril. The pending danger to the planet itself has left the aliens stunned, heart-broken, yet—in spite of this—they attempt to observe non-emotionally.

We ask you not to believe, but to feel. If the belief in the Illuminati or aliens is too much to take, it is nevertheless the story, the mythology of our times. It expresses the archetypal situation we are in, the place of feeling that gives birth to the superhero.

THE BEST PLANET EVER

The beings whom Riley calls the Biaviians are from one of the planetary systems in the Taurus constellation. Their planet, Biaveh, has an eighteen-thousand-mile circumference, so it is slightly smaller than the Earth. But it is a paradise; it is Utopia. They did it. They actually came to a collective state of self-awareness, of consciousness. They got out of a state of conflict with each other, and out of conflict within themselves, and they moved into a self-regulating cycle of ascension and enlightenment. They decided to ennoble life on their planet. Now they have taken their entire culture, and all of their technology, and are journeying across the cosmos, checking it all out with their fleet of Motherships. This appears to be an actual fact, as best as we can understand it, given our rudimentary knowledge of our overall place in the cosmos.

Let's go into our feelings and see how we feel about the idea of our ultimate ascension into the stars, into God's celestial realms that await us—our ascension into Heaven. This is not about believing—that is all gone now. It is beyond belief, actually. It is all about feeling. Consider the idea of a race of beings coming into consciousness, building starships, exploring every facet of life throughout the galaxy, and researching how big God really is. What do you feel when you come into communion with that idea?

With all this in mind, don't we want the best planet? No alien planet is better than ours; we've got the best planet ever. We can take our competitive natures and convert this behavior to something that is beneficial to everybody and everything. And this race of beings from another world has done that. They have moved completely beyond conflict. What a concept! Just that ideal is incredible. Imagine our own planet transcending war, transcending conflict, solving every ecological threat, curing every disease, and embracing harmony in every way imaginable, then moving into the "Star Trek" reality we know is our destiny. All the information and technology to do this are already here right now!

We are heading to a concrescence, an imminent meeting with our future. We believe we are going to be successful and get to paradise. But you never know—the mystery keeps the future veiled. Massively exciting yet intensely challenging times await.

As we open to the perception of human interface with beings from other worlds and sense the boundaries of the playing fields of life widening, we are well advised to remain emotionally and psychically grounded by focusing on core principles. By applying the philosophies outlined in *The Nine Principles of Living in Natural Magic* we come more and more into a harmonic resonance with the immense song of creation, and we get to experience the Almighty blessings of Grace that are sure to carry us forward in safety and wonder.

All the concepts in this book are designed as tools to help us reach our enlightened future. The alien presence alone transforms our awareness. We are not talking about science fiction and video games. These are extraordinary concepts we are exploring here. The advent of what it means to be truly human is at hand. If you dare to dream, now dare to live. Acknowledge the presence of Grace. Be intimate with it in your sincerity. Breathe that Grace with stalwart commitment into every moment. Widen your vision and, by the way, hold onto your chakras, because the future is going to be wildest ride ever.

The Seven Principles of Huna

During our research we came across a priceless formula, an amazing set of principles that form the central core of *The Nine Principles of Living in Natural Magic*. The Seven Principles of Huna (which we incorporate as Principles #2–8 of the 9) are great shamanic canons, originating from Hawaii, interpreted and developed through the work of researchers from Western culture, among them Max Freedom Long. These principles come alive and are seen in every religious practice; they work their way into every shamanic tradition. This is because the traditions and principles of Huna are beautifully basic and universally active.

We (the authors) may not be educated *kahunas* (the Hawaiian title for a priest, expert, or teacher), but we are residents of sacred zones in Hawaii and we are investigators of universal truth—spiritual warriors upon a yogic path. We recognize the importance of communicating the transformed Huna system. Therefore, the central core elements of *The Nine Principles of Living in Natural Magic* are drawn from Hawaii.

As we introduce the Seven Principles of Huna, it is good to understand that this system is a perfect model that reflects a universal principle: *The simpler things are, the easier it is to live.* At this point, with the persistent overload of our senses, we have to keep things simple. If any concept is not simple, we may have difficulty remembering it, and therefore the concept is not useful. So these Huna ideas are distilled into simple sentences, one sentence per principle. And one beautiful Hawaiian word encapsulates each idea.

The Seven Principles of Huna allow us to understand and anchor the state of *Amazing Grace* in a practical, structured way that our logical mind enjoys. The precepts continue beyond that as they help guide us into developing ourselves as heart-centered beings, with activated souls, enlightened minds, and an increasingly healthy biology.

The Seven Principles of Huna can be reapplied to any religious or spiritual system. The principles are open, accepting, and inspire us with concepts of universal wisdom that anyone can embrace.

The ancient Hawaiian pre-warrior tribal cultures were all governed according to the Huna principles. These were not written laws, these were insights into the cosmic order.

We discuss each precept, one at a time. The seven principles are as follows ...

1. IKE—*We Make Our Reality*

The world is what we think it is.

"Hence I have yielded to magic to see ...
what secret force hides in the world and rules its course."
—JOHANN WOLFGANG VON GOETHE, *FAUST*

With *IKE* the individual accepts responsibility for his or her life. Our Creator has given us all the tools to sculpt our experiences in this (and every) life.

THE PRIMARY CONSIDERATION

The primary consideration of *IKE* is a secret single thing you entirely control at every moment and always have. This one thing is truly the symbol of your spirit. This one thing heals you and makes you well all the days of your life. This one thing, when you realize its power, is actually the wellspring of all abundance.

This one thing is your *attitude*. Attitude is your ship's rudder, connected to the steering wheel, where your soul may control your divine destiny or, to the contrary, where it may let go of the wheel as the ship spins out of control.

Bad attitude, bad results at all times ... it can never be otherwise.

Good attitude, good results.

But here is where the *magic* is. It is why you are reading this book right now: good is not good enough. Not anymore. That is gone. Ready. Here we go ... "the best attitude ever." The first step towards creating our own reality is to approach our creative abilities with the best attitude ever.

THE QUANTUM PERSPECTIVE

This idea of creating our own reality is really a quantum perspective. This perspective includes all aspects of our mysterious universe in light of the new physics, which informs us that most of the material or matter inside our body is "empty space." The distances between atoms in our body are vast, as are the distances between electrons and protons. What allows us to exist is a quantum organizing energy field that comprises who we are. And when each one of us meet and greet each other, we are quantum fields of energy that interface with each other. So all the different levels of our being are interfacing with all the different levels of another being, and all the realities of our being are interfacing with the quantum-perspective realities of another being. This is called *infinite correlation*.

There are an infinite amount of things happening at any given instant of time, and they are all being tracked by every level of the intelligence within our being. This is happening whether we acknowledge it or not, whether we even know about it or not. We are not intelligent, we are intelligence itself.

There is no way the mind can understand the concept of infinite correlation—it is impossible. The mind is too logical, too computational, too rational. The only way we can even come into tune with this aspect of quantum reality is through feeling, through a sense emanating from the heart, an intuition. And intuition always guides us better than logic.

Our true nature as mostly "empty" quantum fields of energy is the current verdict of a physical science that, two hundred years ago, was the most dogmatic, mathematic, rational, and logical of all the sciences. Originally Newtonian physics was the most linear and rigid science; now its heir, quantum physics, is completely on the other side, with the nonlinear and intuitive sciences. And it is indicating to us many profound discoveries that we can incorporate into our lives immediately.

One of these discoveries is in the study of random number generation. Dr. Robert Jahn, author of *Margins of Reality,* is one of many scientists and engineers who have confirmed that there is no such thing as a random number. The observer affects the observed and can influence random number generation in several interesting ways.

Here's an example of what Dr. Jahn discovered: If our thoughts are on the flipping of a coin, and that coin is flipped a hundred times, the amount of *noise* in that system is decreased dramatically. This means that if we flip a coin, we might occasionally get tails, say eight times in a row, or we might occasionally get heads eight times in a row. But if our consciousness is focused on that coin, we won't get runs like this; we'll only get, at most, three or four in a row. The *noise,* a run on one side or another, is dramatically decreased. It's also been found that if we focus and really desire heads (or tails), some people will produce heads (or tails) more often, and in some people, dramatically more. It differs per person. Interestingly enough, the opposite has also been found: in some individuals, when they really want heads, they get tails more. Some people are wired backwards.

When we ask how someone could effect a change in a random number, we quickly see that our reality is forming even *before* each instant, meaning there is truly no "now" or "moment." There is only the eternal flow of what is happening. And, like a river or creek, information can gravitate downstream or levitate upstream (influencing the past and the future).

So we know it's a fact—at the quantum level, *there is actually no certainty at all.* It's all uncertainty; anything can happen at any given moment. Which of course is a certainty itself. So it's *the trickster* energy of the shaman in the matrix mythology and cosmic nonlinear equation—the spiritual warrior archetype is a mix of Crazy Horse and Jesus and Buddha. We can no longer even talk of the laws of nature anymore, because they are really "habits of nature." And psychic phenomena, quantum phenomena, absurd synchronicities, and other anomalous happenings can break a habit of nature. As we know, there are always exceptions to the rules. Such exceptions do not happen all the time, but they happen enough, especially when you seek them. It seems that as we are around more beings, places, and things that possess greater *MANA* ("All power comes from within") the chances increase of a sudden event occurring that is clearly not rational or even possible.

MORE ON THE X-FACTOR

How is Nick Good able to carry a 250-pound man across broken glass bottles in his bare feet? How is our friend Howard Wills,[4] gifted with wondrous psychic powers, able to heal a sixteen-year-young boy born crippled with cerebral palsy and multiple sclerosis who suddenly becomes able to walk? How is someone who has never walked a day in his life without crutches and braces able to walk unaided? How is Howard able, in a few minutes, to allow that individual to get up and walk? That is impossible. But it happened. In fact, this type of phenomenon is happening all the time all over the world. From the understanding of the potential of miracles or *hypersynchronicities* we gain an understanding that no disease is terminal, that there is no situation with no way out; *there is always a choice and a chance.* And if we cannot wrap our mind around that concept, we don't need to. All we need to know is that we can open our heart to the possibility that an X-factor is built into everything.

The X-factor can, at any moment, precipitate an impossible event. This is *IKE— we create our own reality.* When all else is left up to us, and we don't know what to do or where to go, we can choose the X-factor. We can pray for the miracle (thought); we can ask for the miracle (word); we can take action towards the miracle (deed)—and we move into the joy, bliss, gratitude, and the peace state we associate with the accomplishment of the invoked miracle (feeling).

Be aware. That's the first thing: awareness. If we are not aware of the X-factor, then we cannot create it, draw from it, focus on it, or do anything related to its magic. This is an awareness that understands that there is uncertainty built into every nook and cranny of reality.

THE WORLD IS WHAT WE BELIEVE IT IS

Central to our human belief systems and the root of all ideas, the hub of all our thoughts, is our sense of identity. In other words, *who I believe I am* defines the way in which I create my world. If, for example, I believe myself to be only a physical body with a limited time span surrounded by the specter of inevitable suffering, then my whole basis (bias) of thought is going to be entirely different than if I believe I am an individual who knows myself to be *an immortal yogi superhero who is having the best day ever.*

Whatever images and feelings, either memories or imaginings, we have in our minds and hearts define the quality and nature of the world we see around us. We know from even rudimentary and preliminary investigations into quantum physics that our external reality is a manifestation of the inner human condition. *Nothing on the outside can change for us until the inner shift has occurred.*

Given enough time and space with a little help from *Amazing Grace,* we do eventually become who we imagine ourselves to be. And the world too becomes what we imagine it to be.

☯

THE BEST REALITY EVER

As long as we are aware that we create our own reality, we might as well create the best reality ever.

There are two ways to do this:

1. Manifest goals and add them to your current reality to make it the best ever.

2. Reinterpret your current reality to make it the best ever.

Creating your own reality means becoming clear about what reality actually is through the lens of innocent perception. Reality is not what is happening to you; it is you happening to the universe. Creating your own reality is not just about manifesting goals (new things) but, in fact, has much to do with really appreciating and then rediscovering the old things. It means realigning the inner interpretations of our current reality through the consciousness of a newborn child.

෧/෧

HOW TO GAMBLE

DAVID: When I was on the Howard Stern radio show a number of years ago, I realized why Howard was at the top of his field. We were engaged in a conversation over the air that was witty, funny, and in general, very good radio. However, instead of being content with that, Howard took a chance and, out of the blue, started taking random callers. The gamble worked and the content of the show jumped to a level of absurd comedy. That is when I realized what it takes to be the best ever.

When the world presents you with the best, gamble it to make it the best ever.

I originally learned this from a friend of the family who was almost fifty years older than me. She told me that she used to gamble on video poker in the big casinos and had discovered a trick to win big. Whenever she had a really great hand, such as a full house, guaranteed to win good money on the machine, she would throw the pair of cards away and go for four of a kind or even five of a kind if there was a wild card in the deck. Using this technique, she often won $10,000 or even $50,000 from these machines. Essentially, she risked throwing away the best hand in exchange for achieving the best hand ever!

෧/෧

THE TOOLS OF MANIFESTATION

Through our thoughts, words, and actions we tap into the magical fabric of life. Thoughts, words, and actions are tools that have a vibratory impact upon the central aethers of the space that surrounds us and permeates everything. *These tools constantly shape and magnetize our reality.*

The idea, then, is to engage the tools of thoughts, words, and actions that immediately and residually create positive, loving, constructive *feelings*. When our focus is on our feeling experience then we can wisely guide our thoughts, words, and actions to where we want to go—into deeper and deeper realms of happiness, bliss, joy, laughter, love, friendship, wonder, and awe.

Essentially, the feelings we experience habitually create our experience of reality.

How do you feel now?

How do you usually feel?

Our feeling experience defines our beliefs, structures, success potential, our home, our work, our relationships—our reality.

Our friend Howard Wills, who is an amazingly gifted healer, has shared with us that his whole approach is through feeling.

The approach to life through feeling is beyond belief and belief systems, it is outside doubt, it is away from all of that—and pessimism is blown out of the picture completely. This new approach to life is about complete certainty based upon feeling. We ask you again: How are you feeling? And if you use this as your guide, then you start coming into tune with the idea that how you are feeling is actually how your *heart* is directing you.

◎⁄◎

2. MAKIA—*Energy Flows Where Attention Goes*

The second principle of Huna is a concept called *MAKIA*. It means: energy flows where attention goes. This concept indicates that we must be aware of our focus. We should be mindful of what we put our attention on, because whatever we put our attention on immediately amplifies and surrounds itself with our thoughts, words, and deeds. Thought-forms accumulate with other thought-forms of a similar vibratory nature.

To achieve our goals we must stay on target. Our experience indicates that the foundation of a true master is the ability to control one's thoughts, and to direct those thoughts in a focused way to the highest and purest considerations.

We've had the privilege of meeting some of the world's most incredible psychics and spiritual healers. The questions we always ask them are: What turns the power on? How does it work? How do you bend that spoon? What do you have to do to activate healing energies? Here's what the answer always is: "I just have to put my attention on it." Again, energy flows where attention goes.

Some people are able to manifest more with their attention than others. Some people have stronger psychic powers than others, and some people are capable of manifesting more extreme synchronicities than others. This appears to be due to each individual's station in their soul's journey. Most of us have been confronted with unresolved burdens (karma of our own doing or from our lineage) or challenging life lessons that have been a damper or an obstacle to living a fully potent life. And yet some people seemed to have blown through all or most of their resistances, as if they have cleared out a log-jammed river. This appears to have much to do with the directing of one's attention away from one's burdens (karma) and onto one's goals.

THE POWER OF WRITING

There is a soul technology that we know for a fact increases the speed of manifestation for everyone, and that is *to simply write things down*. Write down your goals and plans and you immediately and power-fully influence reality. A written goal is able maintain the focus of our attention like a laser. It is a way of gaining leverage on the universe. Anais Nin said, "If it is not written down, it doesn't exist." When you write something down, you activate powerful, invisible forces.

Consider the wizard archetype: The magic words are inscribed. The words are runes—symbols. Every letter is an organized pattern or song. Written words are literally "spells." The act of writing invokes the universe's hidden manifestation powers.

@@

DAVID: Both my brother and I attended *Supercamp* the summer when I was fourteen. (*Supercamp* is a summer camp that teaches accelerated learning and success skills.) This was 1984. This is when and where I first met success guru and friend Anthony Robbins. It is one of the places where Robbins launched his career.

Although I did not keep going to *Supercamp* every year, my brother stayed with it each summer and accumulated *Supercamp* educational materials. Some of these included audiotapes of Anthony Robbins lectures. One of these audiotapes was a goal-setting workshop.

One day I found this tape at my mom's house. I decided to play it. Suddenly I was transported there. In that workshop Robbins had everyone set their goals. So they all did their goal-setting, wrote them down, and then he had people share a few of their goals. He was teach-ing the power of writing down a goal, and then sharing it out loud. Well, a young couple shared the goal that they were going to win the lottery. And Robbins resisted and essentially said, "You can't write a goal down like that, that's impossible." He wanted more realistic goals that could be achieved. And yet the couple insisted and said something to the effect of, "No, we want to keep this as our goal, we're writing it down, you told us to do this, and we believe we can do it." Well, several months later, they won the lottery. That is when I started writing down goals.

⊙⊚

Energy flows where attention goes. When you write something down, you are ordering from the menu of the universe. You can select anything. Think about it. Reflect for a moment on the quantum reality, the infinite correlation to the quantum field. Think about how many cells are resonating right now in your body, communicating with each other. Think of the consciousness of your entire lineage in your cells right now. Think of the memory of just yesterday in your cells right now. When you start adding this up, it's absolutely infinite, every second, what's going on. We're not even getting 0.00000000000000000001% of what's happening in a moment flashing across our consciousness. But when we order on the menu of the universe, by writing something down, a magic event occurs: we begin to consciously select out of an infinite number of choices where we will place our attention.

Goal-setting is a technology. It is a way of gaining leverage on the universe. Writing goals down is a way of amplifying a prayer.

In any situation, at any instant, during the mystery of a sudden opportunity for a prepared goal-oriented individual, the direction is revealed and a way is shown.

It appears that the world makes way for those who know where they are going. As you write down your goals, you are telling God, or the Creator, or Nature, or "Infinite Intelligence" which way you are going.

Take heed of the tried and true saying behind the goal-setting gurus: "You must be specific to be terrific." The more specific we are about our goal, the more focused is our attention. Our goal should also be in the present tense, as if it is happening now. Additionally, our goal should be positively framed, as something we are moving towards not away from.

HOW TO SET TECHNOLOGICALLY SUPERIOR GOALS

EXAMPLE:

Technologically Incorrect Goal:

I hope I will get rid of my junky car.

Analysis:

This goal is in the future (I will). This goal doesn't state the goal (what one is moving towards); it contains what one is moving away from (the junky car).

Technologically Correct Goal:

I drive a brand-new hybrid vehicle that gets great gas mileage.

Analysis:

This goal is technically correct.

Technologically Superior Goal:

I drive the best ever brand-new hybrid vehicle that gets the best gas mileage ever.

Analysis:

This goal, by using the word "ever" a couple of times, opens the delivery of the content of the goal to divine powers outside one's self. Remember, words are invocations, words have weight.

EXAMPLE:

Technologically Incorrect Goal:

I am going to get out of this terrible relationship.

Analysis:

This goal is in the future (I am going to). This goal doesn't state the goal (what one is moving towards); it contains what one is moving away from (a terrible relationship).

Technologically Correct Goal:

I have a great relationship with the partner of my dreams.

Analysis:

This goal is technically correct.

Technologically Superior Goal:

I have the best relationship ever with a partner who is beyond my wildest dreams.

Analysis:

This goal, by using the words "ever" and "beyond," opens the delivery of the content of the goal to divine powers outside one's self.

EXAMPLE:

Technologically Incorrect Goal:

I need to lose weight.

Analysis:

This goal is in the future (I need to). This goal doesn't state the goal (what one is moving towards); it contains only a problem (needing to lose weight).

Technologically Correct Goal:

I have achieved my ideal weight of 110 pounds (50 kg) swiftly and efficiently.

Analysis:

This goal is technically correct.

Technologically Superior Goal:

I am always at the best weight ever for myself and I instantly achieve and maintain that weight in any situation forever.

Analysis:

This goal, by using the words "ever" and "forever," opens the delivery of the content of the goal to divine powers outside one's self.

ᢙᠥᢙ

EXAMPLE:

Technologically Incorrect Goal:

I will not feel bad.

Analysis:

This goal is in the future (I will). This goal doesn't state the goal (what one is moving towards); it contains what one is moving away from (feeling bad).

Technologically Correct Goal:

I feel great all the time.

Analysis:

This goal is technically correct. This is also the most powerful type of goal—a way-of-being goal.

Technologically Superior Goal:

I effervesce with the most radiance, joy, and health, and I consistently feel the best ever.

Analysis:

This goal, by using the word "ever," opens the delivery of the content of the goal to divine powers outside one's self. As we have seen in previous examples, this is the most powerful type of goal because it is a way-of-being goal.

Writing things creates awareness. Sometimes simple awareness is all that is needed. Barbara Brown, in her book *Supermind: The Ultimate Energy,* recounts a study in which chronic headache sufferers were asked to keep a diary of the frequency and severity of their headaches. Although the record was intended to be a first step in preparing the headache sufferers for further treatment, most of the subjects found that when they began to keep a diary, their headaches disappeared.

Goal-setting is ultimately about deciding how you will deal with life's issues in advance. You can write your story down *ahead of time* to experience it the way you want it.

DAVID: I have written down goals that I completely planned—things I planned to do on a trip that were arranged to happen a certain way. And when those plans fell apart, I just kept moving forward and found the goal would still be achieved by totally unexpected, even startling, means. This has been enough for me to move from believing to actually knowing that written goals invoke the powers of the universe.

My belief is that simply writing down a goal is often enough to give it momentum into the universe and create the outcome.

Because I am aware of the shocking power of setting goals, goal-setting is a party, a treat for me, and a wonderful break from my daily schedule.

Now this question comes up frequently: Can you write your goals down with your computer? And the answer appears to be, yes. That's been my experience. I have been doing it both ways (writing goals by hand and by computer) for more than fifteen years now.

When people have goals but do not write them down, they are simply kidding themselves. Conversely, when people have the courage to write their goals down, then in that moment they are saying to the universe that they believe these things can come true, that they are possible. Immediately in that moment the invisible forces come to their aid. The act of simply setting a goal is an act of faith.

While science operates on practical theories built around things that can be seen, touched, felt, and manipulated, the art of goal achievement operates on an additional principle. Its power is potentiated only when the goal is believed and taken to heart with the power of faith. This is where quantum leaps happen in consciousness.

Faith is central to all of life. We have seen that disbelievers (those who say they have no faith, those for whom only seeing is believing) will go to a doctor whose name they cannot pronounce and whose degrees they have never verified to receive a prescription they cannot read and which they take to a pharmacist they do not know. They receive a chemical compound they cannot understand which they consume daily according to arbitrary instructions ... all in trusting, sincere faith!

If one can truly find a basis for high faith—the place in your heart to trust in yourself and the future—then great goal achievements are possible.

DAVID: Why do we want anything in life? Why do we want the perfect relationship? Why do we want to be at our ideal weight? Why do we want success? Why do we want achievement? Why would we want a million dollars? We don't want a million dollars for the million dollars. We don't want a vacation in Hawaii for the vacation. We don't want a beautiful home and garden for its looks. We really want all those things because of how we think those things will make us feel. We think these achievements will make us happy, joyous, blissful, fulfilled, ecstatic, peaceful, etc. Is that fair? Now, almost nobody realizes that you can have happiness, joy, bliss, etc., simply by setting goals to be in such states. We call these types of goals "ways-of-being goals." Instead of devising a strategy to go to Hawaii on a vacation in order to feel blissful, why not cut to the chase and create a goal to feel blissful all the time? This is exactly the path on which goal-setting has taken me in my life. Why should I wait to be happy later when I can be happy now? "I am the happiest person ever" is a "way-of-being" goal. A way-of-being goal can occur for no reason and can be manifested instantly.

By transforming our way of being to the highest states through goal-setting, we automatically set up the prerequisite for the achievement of any "person, place, or thing" goal, because the type of person you are will determine to a large degree how readily you can manifest any person, place, or thing. The happier, more blissful, and more ecstatic a person you are, the more attractive and charismatic you are and the easier you manifest anything you select. Ultimately success is not something you achieve; it is who you are, it is a way of being.

☺⁄☺

Goal-setting is a day-to-day process. It is called a "To Do" list. From a practical standpoint in everyday life: run the day or the day runs you. Plan each day in advance and then execute the plan. The idea is to get the list down on paper or computer before each day begins.

No business could run without things being written down. Certainly your life is more important than any business—so write every plan, every preferred outcome, every goal in your journal or computer.

Keep goal-setting and achievement fun and exploratory. With graceful determination, plan the most healthful, most thrilling, most romantic, and most spiritual year of your life. In fact, through goal-setting, plan the best life ever!

GO WITH THE FLOW

The proper superhero is a "flowist"—one who goes with the flow. Allow the natural flow to occur and accelerate towards goals wisely when events show up in favor of those goals. Nurture yourself as you pursue your goals through loving and compassionate feelings. There is no rush, everything comes in its own time.

Goal-setting and achieving must be carefully balanced with going with the flow. Essentially, you can avoid stress by following synchronicities. Our experience has been that we cannot skip goal-setting and just go with the flow of what's happening. Being lazy opens up the possibility of getting swept away by the collective momentum of others (habits of consciousness). We can work towards our goals, consistently and synchronistically, not rigorously.

By persistently creating momentum towards the creations we have chosen (goals) by thoughts, words, and actions, we can precipitate the manifestation of the goal or goals. We can all learn to live by the metaphor of the tortoise and the hare: "Slow and steady wins the race." Our friend Peter the Gnome says: "The faster you go, the longer it takes and the more it costs you to get there." According to *A Course in Miracles,* infinite patience is the only thing that generates immediate results.

Inspiration and Goals

When we are inspired about something, something we love, time goes away and disappears. Because of the amount of energy that flows into the moment, there's no more thought of food, there's no more thought of anything else. . . . It just all goes away. So, energy flows where attention goes and is amplified when we narrow this funnel down and write goals and dreams that inspire us. And when we start writing these inspirational goals and achieving them, we open the floodgates. We open the valves of abundance completely as we totally recognize who we are, how we operate, and why we are here. When we line up completely and totally with the inspiration of our mission in life, eternal abundance rains upon us.

Minimum Optimum

We recommend that you keep your goals close at hand, written down and easily accessed so you can look at these as often as possible each week. We recommend that you condense your entire life mission into one statement, a mantra, or a couple of words. We recommend that you place all your goals into one computer file, under one phrase, such as: "The Best Goals Ever." You can then take your file, which contains all of your goals and your mission, and meditate at a certain time each day on manifesting the entire content of this file. Meditating on the entire content of your goal file does not mean you have to review every goal; it simply means you meditate on the goal file. Why does this work? *Because everything's made up anyway.* You might as well make it up how you want it. Make it easy, efficient. The easy way is to put all your goals into one file and just meditate upon that file. In fact, during the sunrise or sunset, in addition to meditating on your goals file, you can also do yoga, chi gong, mantras, and prayers while you focus your eyes on the first one to ten minutes of the rising sun and/or the last one to fifteen minutes of the setting sun. This is an outstanding "minimum optimum" approach to successful living. Looking at the sun for a few minutes each day at sunrise or sunset resets your circadian rhythms and gives you more energy.

In essence, *MAKIA* informs us of a new, technologically upgraded approach to goal-setting. *MAKIA* transforms your meditation into a laser beam of focus condensed to the simplest point (your goal file).

Overall, the minimum optimum approach draws the principle of *MAKIA* into the following useful formula:

1. Know your goals inside and out via review and rewriting. Record your visions. Develop, in writing, the action plans.

2. Take action. Self-discipline is the ability to make yourself do what you should do, when you should do it, whether you feel like it or not. Use your laser-beam focus.

3. Be aware if your actions are bringing you closer to or farther away from your goals.

4. Be flexible. Refine your approach until you get the results you're looking for. Use the Trial and Success Method: Learn from your successes and adjust your behavior accordingly.

☉/☉

NICK: Successful goal-setting. Taking it to the next level. That is what we are doing here.

What are your goals? Have you made up your mind? Is that mind powered by unshakable invincibility emanating from the depth of the soul? Are you SUNstoppable?

My life experience has demonstrated to me that the only limits are the ones we believe in. Many of those beliefs, in fact most of them, have been wired into our subconscious, primarily before the age of seven. Think about that for a moment. The emotional climate in our mother's womb, our parents' relationship, the family home, the state of the nest, the environment, the culture in which we formed at a very early age are the predominant factors which *have defined our ability to believe in ourselves.* This is phenomenal, significant information. This conditioning doesn't just define our mental states but actually *regulates* the quality of life force flowing into our being. The vibratory recording of thoughts and feelings and actions you expressed, witnessed, and reacted to during the first seven years of your life and ever since are still recorded within you. These recordings, if discordant, prevent us from entering the free flow and really interfacing in harmony with the underlying ever-present Force. These disharmonious recordings, *until they are consciously erased,* are a root causal factor in every disease and stress equation.

I was once given three months to live. I could see the end of the corridor—a choice I had to make. There were two brown doors. It was a corridor in a hospital in England. The smell of my father's rotting corpse, a few days before his funeral, still burned in my nostrils. My brother's death six weeks after Dad was like acid poured on my soul. I was deafened by the loud SNAP! in my head on the day of his passing. As a broken-hearted man, I chose to walk out the doors of that hospital, and more than a decade later I am sharing this tale with you. The power of goal-setting saved me. I used to write my goals on the ceiling above the bed in which I slept. They were all in present tense. "I am a super-healthy, super-happy, super-successful embodiment of peace, love, and joy. I cannot be stopped!"

I was born into a violent, sad home full of judgment and denial. The local society was just as violent and judgmental. My mother could smoke forty cigarettes every day and my father sixty or eighty. They were both whiskey drinkers; they didn't get along. Anger and tears were the prevalent weather. I was born in the aftermath of my older brother's death. Can you imagine the environment in that womb? The vibrations of deformity in there? The opportunity to capitulate, to lack self-belief, to conform to distorted, disharmonious, and toxic conditioning? That was the root of my disease. The program was erased and I am still alive today.

Goal-setting is something I have been doing consciously for twenty-five years and more. Overcoming the odds, living mini miracles. Perhaps you have too, maybe not all the time consciously, but investing energy in the mechanism. Achieving goals is fun and a critical skill to be proficient in.

Vision. Plan. Action. That is the formula. Enter into the associated feeling states of your desired outcome. Pray as if you have already received the thing—that's the way to get results. Trim, adjust your strategies for acting out the attainment of the goal, and stick to the plan. Vision early morning and night. Say YES! and clap your hands. Encode your goal file with a trigger word and seed that word into your psyche on a subconscious level, especially before sleeping. Create picture boards of your end results. Be sure that your goals totally align with your unique mission and purpose. When utilizing our *Success Ultra Now Inner Journey Audio Program (SUNPOP),* you can then receive assistance in lining up your soul's mission with the overall collective vision of heaven on Earth. With *SUNPOP* we have taken goal realization to the most extraordinary level.

Raise your sights, dare to embrace the vision of who you truly are: a cosmic being expressing yourself in an ocean of eternity, frozen in the world of form, temporarily perhaps, on the verge of freedom, on a mission to become the embodiment of the living solution.

"What you think upon grows. Whatever you allow to occupy your mind you magnify in your life. Whether the subject of your thought is good or bad, the law works, and the condition grows. Any subject that you keep out of your mind tends to diminish in your life, because what you do not use atrophies. The more you think of grievances, the more such trials you will continue to receive; the more you think of the good fortune you have had, the more good fortune will come to you."

—EMMET FOX

3. MANA—*All Power Comes from Within*

"There is a variable schism which seethes the marrow of infinity, and we ever seek to raise our lips to suckle the nectar of its Omsa."
—O-QUA TANGIN WANN (A.K.A. TAN)

The third principle of Huna is known as *MANA*—all power comes from within. Recall, the Africans aboard Captain John Newton's slave ship. Shackled to the floor below deck, seasick, soul-weary, and trapped in an impossible situation. Yet, in spite of the close proximity of a terrible death, they were able to draw upon *MANA*—the power that always resides somewhere deep inside.

It is never too late. Even when you have given everything you have got, there is always something left. More and more we are being called to summon this power within. To do this we must be able to tap that potent natural resource that is an ocean which laps against the shores of our own soul. That ocean is our physical body. Its ability to transmit soul power into this reality is dependent on the art of nutrition. Not just any old nutrition, but what the superhero archetype requests— the best nutrition ever.

"You are what you eat" connotes a holy relationship—a holy communion with the greater part of ourselves. "You are what you eat" is a zip file we were given when incarnated that can guide us, strengthen us, remake us anew, unfold when needed, and assist our sacred journey. The superhero understands this at the depth of her/his soul and immediately selects to avoid all pesticide-sprayed, larvicide-soaked, fungicide-washed, herbicide-dipped, suicide-filled, chemically fertilized, genetically modified, hormonally altered, *E. coli* contaminated, greedy substances that are currently called "food." The superhero, upon becoming aware, immediately selects a diet rich in raw, organic, living foods. These foods include:

> Fruits
> Vegetables
> Nuts
> Seeds
> Seaweeds
> Sprouts
> Grasses (wheatgrass, etc.)
> Herbs
> Superfoods

(For more details on raw, organic, living-food diets, please read David Wolfe's books: *Eating for Beauty, The Sunfood Diet Success System,* and *Naked Chocolate.*)

Coupled with these food choices we offer deep recognition to history's leading genius hearts, master herbalists, and agricultural artists (including Rudolf Steiner, Julius Hensel with his *Bread from Stones,* Dr. Maynard Murray with his *Sea Energy Agriculture,* as well as hundreds of others). These remarkable individuals have given us the keys to the best nutrition ever; they have given us the understanding that love-filled intention and high mineral-content food is the basis of wholesome nutrition. If the soil is rich with love-filled intention and minerals by the application of powdered rocks, river silt, ocean water residues, Dead Sea salt extracts, etc., the food grown therein will be superior in vitamins, minerals, enzymes, protein, polysaccharides, oils, and immune system-, skeletal-, as well as nervous system-supporting nutrients.

Their knowledge in combination with the living, superfood diet now links into one of the greatest scientific re-discoveries of our time— the re-discovery of an entirely new class of mineral substances that are deeply associated with life-force energy, consciousness, and super powers.

The following discussion opens cracks in the floors of the hallowed halls of present-day science's mis-understandings, and it allows you to take immediate agricultural and dietary advantage of this momentous discovery.

MANA is a Hawaiian word (also a Hebrew-Egyptian word) meaning power and life force, and it appears to have the identical meaning as the Sanskrit word *prana*. Others have used the term *MANA* interchangeably with terms such as life force, energy, breath, spirit, vitality, wind, and strength. *MANA* is said to work on, in, and around us.

We, however, identify *MANA* not in an exotic or exclusively esoteric way, but as a class of physically distinct atomic mineral substances that are unique forms of matter that appear to be closer to the state of aether or vacuum or pure energy than normal matter such as the common mineral and atomic compounds found on Mendeleyev's Periodic Table of the Elements. These distinct substances also seem to be intimately woven into the fabric of living things. They appear to be associated with what causes everything to "live." These forms of matter can have an attraction for the heavens, and through proper forms of motion and catalysts, they will aetherialize and levitate (or actually fall upwards). Such substances in spiral motion and in combination with hydrogen and sulfur compounds could be the cause of all plant and animal growth upward against gravity (we believe they can, under controlled scientific conditions, actually displace the force of gravity, thus causing levitation). These substances are not like the other atomic units of matter found on the Periodic Table of the Elements. When isolated and separated from other parent materials, these substances display consciousness. They move to escape isolation by jumping (or teleporting) into nearby salts, oils, water sources, and even the atmosphere itself.

On the Internet, these substances are not called *MANA;* they are called *Ormus* (sometimes also referred to as ORME, monoatomic elements, and/or m-state materials). In our definition Ormus and *MANA* mean the same thing and we use them interchangeably. Ormus atoms or minerals are a chemically identified separate class of substances, just like the halogens or the metals, except that Ormus atoms do not find placement on the two-dimensional Periodic Table of the Elements. Ormus elements appear to be isolated or micro-cluster bits of atomic materials that are closer, as previously mentioned, to the pure energy state of the vacuum (aether or zero point). Ormus elements can have the visible appearance (when isolated and dried) of silicon-like, ceramic powdery substances.

Ormus elements apparently show up in our reality (deep in the Earth, in lava, in salts, in the oceans, in springs, etc.) as infolded substances that, under certain types of stimulation, will unfold into a metal. Ormus could be the source of all metals. Therefore, we identify the Ormus elements in relationship to the metal they can unfold into (e.g. Ormus copper, Ormus gold, Ormus rhodium, etc.).

This brings us to an interesting immediate supposition: what if the whole Periodic Table of the Elements, the scientific cataloging of the atoms (hydrogen, helium, carbon, oxygen, sulfur, nitrogen, calcium, iodine, gold, etc.) is incomplete? Then everything we were taught about the atomic content of water, stones, precious minerals, gems, crystals, plants, animals, etc., is incomplete.

It has been discovered in this regard that what is being called carbon is actually not always carbon; sometimes it is something else. What is being called calcium is actually not always calcium; sometimes it is something else. What is being called silicon is actually not always silicon; sometimes it is something else. What is being called iron sometimes is actually not always iron; sometimes it is something else. And that something else is actually *MANA* (Ormus).

This material is found inside of every human being. David Hudson, a present-day alchemist who "re-discovered" Ormus in basalt rock in the Arizona desert, indicates that as much as 5% of the dry matter weight of our nervous system could be Ormus elements (in particular: Ormus rhodium and Ormus iridium) based on Ormus extractions he conducted on calf and pig brains.

As the current Internet-Ormus theory has it, Ormus elements are the bridge for what brings light into your body. They literally feed your light body. They are an intimate part of what causes you to be conscious.

The rediscovery of Ormus in our times by alchemist David Radius Hudson appears to be one of the greatest scientific breakthroughs ever; it has revivified and given new meaning to history's great alchemical writings.

Because of the dynamic nature of communication in our times, David Hudson's information (as recorded and transcribed during his famous lectures for audiences in Dallas, Yelm, Vancouver, and Global Sciences, which are available on the Internet) reveals alchemical secrets in a format that is understandable and useful to the layperson as well as the curious home scientist or mild-mannered superhero.

David Hudson made some innovative discoveries. He found that Ormus minerals are present in animals, plants, and in the soil of the Earth itself in varying concentrations. Hudson also discovered that Ormus may be ten times more abundant in human tissues than all trace minerals (e.g. zinc, copper, iodine, chromium, etc.) combined. The implications of all this, as it pertains to nutrition, become obvious. What if we have been deficient in Ormus minerals? What if we've been taking the wrong kind of mineral supplements? Is it possible that we (and our ancestors) have never been filled to the brim with Ormus minerals? And therefore never achieved our full capabilities of personal power?

Hudson's research led to the theory that Ormus elements can be accumulated by individuals who ingest Ormus in various forms (food, concentrated supplements, atmospheric sources, fresh spring water at the source, through the skin, psychically-meditatively). Ormus can also be excreted.

We suspect that Ormus can be accumulated and excreted from

two types of evidence: 1) We find that the physical effects felt by those who take Ormus mineral supplements appear to accumulate. 2) Ormus elements can be extracted from urine. Therefore, it is reasonable to conclude that the content of Ormus elements in the human body is dynamic, not stable.

We have found and collected data over a number years indicating that certain plants either "mine" and sequester Ormus elements within their living cells in higher densities than other plants or concentrate them in high quantities in ways that other plants do not. Even though this list is far from complete (and very rudimentary), we can now say with relative certainty that the Ormus-rich plants and edibles include:

Almonds

Aloe vera

Apricot kernels (the inner pit of the stone)

Bee pollen (wild, especially from volcanic regions)

Bloodroot

Blue-green algae from Klamath Lake, Oregon

Carrots (depends on the Ormus content of the soil)

Chamae Rose

Chocolate (organic chocolate contains Ormus nickel)

Coconut water (wild)

Flax oil

Garlic

Goji berries (in the polysaccharides)

Grasses and grains (if grown with diluted ocean water or with the proper fertilizer; grasses and grains include wheat, barley, corn, rice, sugar cane, etc.)

Grape seeds

Honey (wild, especially from volcanic regions)

Larch bark

Medicinal mushrooms (reishi, cordyceps, coriolus, *Fomes fomentarius,* shiitake, maitake, etc.)

Mustard (brown and stone-ground)
Noni fruit
Propolis
Royal jelly
Shark cartilage
Sheep sorrel
Slippery elm bark
St. John's Wort
Vanilla (whole beans)
Watercress
White pine bark

It is becoming more and more clear that the superfoods and super-herbs of the planet concentrate the Ormus minerals more than other foods. It is possible that future analytical data will support the presence of high Ormus concentrations in spirulina, chlorella, marine phytoplankton, maca, kelp (as well as other seaweeds), hemp (and many other seeds), nettles, asparagus, ginseng, astragalus, ho shou wu (fo-ti), cat's claw bark, pau d'arco bark, tulsi, ashwaganda, tree sap (maple, pine), many of the berries (acai, blueberries, raspberries, black-berries, schizandra, ginseng berries, spikenard berries, goose berries, Incan berries, etc.).

These are the primary foods of the superhero. Imagine the rejuvenation and hydration of every one of your cells. Picture your every cell as a galaxy with a spinning black hole (singularity) at its center and a renewed event horizon (membrane) allowing it to magnetize new energy levels, awarenesses, and cellular attitudes.

In the greatest movie of all the ages it appears that GMO popcorn and high-fructose licorice are going to be replaced by the best food ever.

On his website (www.subtleenergies.com) Barry Carter lists at least six ways to concentrate Ormus out of natural substances in order to create what we will call "Ormus-mineral supplements." We have pioneered at least two additional methods to concentrate Ormus in our laboratory (these were developed and perfected while producing Ormus gold). There are likely many other ways to create Ormus-mineral supplements or concentrates.

By using wood-burning stoves (not electric or gas) and fresh spring water we have demonstrated that during water-heat extractions of certain plant materials (especially tree mushrooms, vanilla, and goji berries), we can extract Ormus containing compounds (polysaccharides) intact into the tea.

☯☯

ALCHEMICAL CONSCIOUSNESS

One of the unwritten rules of alchemy is that the alchemist must consume the products of her/his alchemy in order to completely understand not only what s/he is dealing with, but how to achieve even higher levels of alchemical production.

This is how the great Swiss scientist Albert Hoffman cracked the secret of magic mushrooms. The reason why Hoffman was able to figure out how magic mushrooms worked and why he was able to isolate the primary active chemical compound in magic mushrooms, namely *psilocybin,* is that he was the only scientist on the task who was actually eating the products of his experiments.

☯☯

ORMUS AND ANCIENT EGYPT

According to legend, the ancient Egyptians ingested Ormus elements with frankincense and/or myrrh essential oils. The Egyptians called Ormus "manna" or sometimes, in the *Egyptian Book of the Dead,* "mfkzt," meaning "what is it?" In ancient Hebrew the word "manna" has the same meaning as the sentence "what is it?" According to Hudson, the ascension and spiritualization of the crown prince into the pharaoh involved a nine-month fast on Ormus elements. He speculated that the ascending pharaoh would ingest 500 milligrams of Ormus gold per day!

ORMUS IN THE BIBLE

There are many possible references to Ormus in both the *Torah* and *New Testament*.

❖ It is written in Revelations, "Blessed be the man who will overcome for he shall be given the hidden manna, the white stone of purest kind, upon which will be written a new name." [Revelations 2:17]

❖ Exodus 32:19-20 records the following incident after the Israelites had begun worshipping the golden calf: "And as soon as he came near the camp and saw the calf and the dancing, Moses' anger burned hot, and he threw the tablets out of his hands and broke them at the foot of the mountain. And he took the calf which they had made, and burnt it with fire, and ground it to powder, and scattered it upon the water, and made the people of Israel drink it."

❖ Revelations 21:18-21 mentions something unique about Ormus gold: "The wall was built of jasper, while the city was pure gold, clear as glass. The foundations of the wall of the city were adorned with every jewel; the first was jasper, the second sapphire, the third agate, the fourth emerald, the fifth onyx, the sixth carnelian, the seventh chrysolite, the eighth beryl, the ninth topaz, the tenth chrysoprase, the eleventh jacinth, the twelfth amethyst. And the twelve gates were twelve pearls, each of the gates made of a single pearl, and the street of the city was pure gold, transparent as glass." David Hudson discovered that Ormus gold could be annealed into a clear glass and speculated that the capstone of the Great Pyramid at Giza may have been made of Ormus gold glass.

◉◉

From what we have learned so far, we see that knowledge of our hidden *MANA* is revolutionary. Ormus may be understood as the wire that connects our consciousness to the inner network of pure energy and imagination. This has been called various names by different thinkers: Infinite Intelligence, the oversoul, the implicate order, eternal consciousness, the Akashic Records, etc. Stated another way, *Ormus elements are the physical substances that most easily access the non-physical matrix of eternal consciousness.*

Based on our current knowledge about Ormus and the *function* of Ormus in living cells, we feel secure in quoting the following metaphor by Barry Carter:

"It is like every cell has a cell phone. These are the Ormus containing structures inside the cell. The Ormus elements themselves, are like the microwave transducers (modem) that connect with the implicate network (Internet). The cell phone's antenna is the DNA, which acts to pull in information from eternal consciousness and resonate it to other cells or cell phones with the same DNA. The landline phone consists of our neurotransmitters and nerves that essentially act as a back-up system to the Ormus cell phone. A malfunction in the Ormus cell-phone system appears to be related to aging, and a malfunction in the landline back-up network appears to be associated with depression."

Now the questions arise: What if our cells have never had the proper cell phone or the best cell phone? What if our DNA could suddenly be repaired and our antennae started to function properly? What if we had enough Ormus saturating our system that every cell in our body began to resonate in perfect harmony? If Ormus elements transduce more energy and information directly into the cell, what is the consequence? The answers to these questions contain the promises and possibilities of Ormus agriculture and superhero nutrition as well as the opportunity of a brilliant and technologically innovative future.

We should be aware (based on the anecdotal evidence of individuals who have spent years consuming Ormus supplements) that Ormus elements will help carry and amplify any thought we think. Therefore a body saturated with Ormus is going to be on a psychic cell phone all the time. We can say anything we want on a cell phone, and it does not respond to the content. Ormus will communicate any content. If we believe that Ormus saturation is the solution, we might take note that positive thinking, paradise goal-setting, beautiful spiritual disciplines of practicing compassion, superheroism, etc.—as well as raw and living-food nutrition—should be considered in conjunction with Ormus supplementation in order to amplify the positivity.

What effects do Ormus elements create in the physical body? Due to the novelty of the subject matter, very little scientific data and studies exist on this subject, most of the research is anecdotal.

According to researcher Laurence Gardner (author of *Lost Secrets of the Sacred Ark*), some tests were conducted by the Alphalearning Institute at the World Trade Center in Lugano, Switzerland. Specialists in behavioral sciences and learning deficiencies such as dyslexia and ADHD gave measured doses of Ormus mineral supplements to ten volunteers—males and females of varying ages. Over a number of weeks, the EEG brain scans showed a significant enhancement of alpha waves, leading to hemispheric left- and right-brain synchronization. This phenomenon facilitates heightened learning ability, memory, creative skills, and lower stress levels.

Barry Carter reports that Ormus copper appears to have an anti-aging effect and is known to reverse gray hair in some people. It has been noted that two years of consistently taking Ormus copper can darken hair color.

Barry Carter has mentioned that his alchemist friend, known as "The Essene," believes that Ormus copper is involved in the working of chlorophyll. This gives us the idea that green leafy vegetables grown in an Ormus-rich environment (watered with ocean water diluted twenty times by distilled water or rain water) should be an excellent source of anti-aging compounds.

We have theorized, based on our own Ormus production experience and experiments, that Ormus gold appears to increase the production of serotonin to affect tryptamine amino acids and neurotransmitters including tryptophan, 5-hydroxy tryptophan, melatonin, and dimethyltryptamine. The overall effect of this seems to enhance a sense of well-being and spiritual harmony. If too much Ormus gold is taken, the body will flip the serotonin into melatonin and one will become sleepy.

☯️

"Unio Mystica—The mystical union of opposites."
—ALCHEMICAL PRINCIPLE

DAVID: My research into Ormus and alchemy has led to the following understanding of how Ormus elements interact dynamically *with other matter.*

Ormus elements are female in nature and want to mate with the Sun's male energies. The Sun's male elements want to mate with the female Ormus elements of the Earth. The Sun's primary male elements include oxygen, ozone, radiation, and Wilhelm Reich's bions (the squiggly, sperm-like, aetherialized objects you see when dark blue and purple colors are present in the atmosphere). Together the female elements attempt to spiral upward and reach the Sun, and the male elements attempt to spiral downward and reach the Earth. These opposites usually meet somewhere near the surface of the Earth and create growth in life. The first-born is dew water, water with no carbon, only Ormus (mother), oxygen (father), and hydrogen (child). The Ormus elements, because they carry the seed of a child (hydrogen), are therefore (in my opinion) more worthy of study than male elements.

The combination of Ormus with solar energies creates growth, as the two are always seeking each other. Ormus is intrinsic to us as humans because we assemble ourselves from the Earth and grow towards the Sun. The solar energies are brought in primarily by breathing. Therefore, individuals who are massively saturated with Ormus elements automatically attract more oxygen and ozone to themselves by breathing than an individual who is depleted of Ormus and unconscious of such forces. That means that Ormus saturation automatically causes more of the proper oxygenation of the tissues and the creation of the purest dew water in the body.

Cooking food on an open flame or with oil or in any way with the presence of oxygen can add so much "solar" energy to Ormus elements that the Ormus will become carbonized and oxidized and therefore less useful nutritionally. Microwaving, irradiating, or using extreme heat with food can flip the Ormus into its metallic state, making it potentially useless or even dangerous.

Although the recommendation is not confirmed scientifically, the Ormus community generally advises against taking sulfur supplements or preservatives (MSM, angstrom sulfur, sulfites, etc.) with Ormus supplements (as opposed to Ormus-rich foods), as the sulfur appears to compete for the same receptor sites as those that the Ormus supplements fit into and/or the sulfur is so high in energy that it reacts with the Ormus supplement, atomically changing it. However, Ormus-rich foods are okay to take with MSM (methyl-sulfonyl-methane) because the Ormus elements are chemically bound into complex molecules and do not react with MSM.

David Hudson noted that toxic sulfur compounds called sulfites (used as a food and beverage preservative) deactivate Ormus elements (move them towards becoming metals).

◎◎

WATER

Water is the key element in the world right now and forever. Water consciousness is our primary ally in the unfoldment of the greatest love story ever told. Falling back in love with water can do more to transform you into a superhero than practically anything else.

D.H. Lawrence wrote: "Water is H_2O, hydrogen two parts, oxygen one part, but there's a third thing that makes it water and nobody knows what that is." We believe that water actually consists of not just three elements (two known and one unknown) but five atomic substances, namely: hydrogen, oxygen, carbon, silicon, and Ormus elements.

A fact that is unknown to most people is that one cannot electrolytically disassociate water without a catalyst (an acid). Water with no electrolytes cannot be electrolytically disassociated into oxygen and hydrogen. Therefore, the actual composition of water is still open to debate. We suspect that during the electrolysis of water and acid, the hydrogen coming off as a gas is not pure hydrogen; it still contains carbon and Ormus elements attached to some of the hydrogen atoms.

According to Barry Carter, triple-distilled water weighs about one pound (0.45 kg) more per gallon (3.8 liters) than chemical water made by burning hydrogen in oxygen. And there are only approximately 8.3 pounds (3.8 kg) per gallon (3.8 liters). Additionally, many chemists know that chemically created water is toxic. We believe that chemical water is toxic because it contains almost no carbon, no silicon, and no Ormus and therefore in its "hunger" will rob those elements from the body in order to become whole.

DAVID: In ninth grade, my chemistry teacher told us not to drink the water we were using in a series of experiments. I asked him why. He said that the water is chemical water (made from pure oxygen and hydrogen gases). He told me that pure H_2O is toxic and would kill you if you drink enough of it. I thought: "H_2O is a poison?" How many people know that? Then what is water? We thought that H_2O was water! This is the basis of our whole science, isn't it? Modern so-called "science," which, from its lack of understanding of vital chemistry, is turning the entire planet into a trash heap, must have some major flaws in its assumptions. The misidentification of water as H_2O appears to be the worst of "science's" ill-conceived theories.

Dr. Masaru Emoto's work presented in the book *The Messages from Water* indicates that something in the water is responding to consciousness instantaneously. It is our contention that this "something" is the Ormus elements inside the water.

We have noted that Ormus-rich, specifically-dense, cold water (39.2 degrees Fahrenheit or 4 degrees Celsius) flows with an oily consistency and a luminous quality (it emits blue light). Ormus, in general, is said to have an oily nature. As discussed, it likes hydrocarbons such as oil. What this means is not certain, but this insight allows you to identify Ormus-rich waters.

Ultimately, we are "children of the living waters." We arise from the level of purity and nobility felt only when one spiritually experiences ice-cold spring waters and creeks emanating from pristine environments or from the glacial-melt caves high in the mountains where the water pours forth with shocking purity.

The ennoblement of water in springs due to contact with the information of below-ground minerals and their eons of unknowable geological history provides you the chance to calibrate the true depth and meaning of purity, love, gratitude, and *MANA*. It is our perception that ice-cold, living waters—especially those emanating from mysterious places such as the Himalaya, the Andes, and in particular, the Canadian shield[4]—embody the highest levels of health, beauty, and love that the Gaia organism can create. Using David Hawkins' kinesiology method for calibrating consciousness (see his book *Power vs. Force*), we have measured certain sacred spring waters to reach levels of consciousness ranging from 2500 to 4000. By contrast, according to Hawkins, Jesus and Buddha measure in at the highest level previously tested for, a level of 1000.

Pure spring water that comes straight out of the earth opens doors for you and gives you a sensory perception of the Ormus elements— *MANA*. You can drink spring water, bathe in it, mist it and breathe it in, carry it with you in a vial, pray over it, or any number of things. All these methods of using water serve to amplify your perception of *MANA*. And in that moment of perception, you may perceive that all of a sudden you do not even need the water anymore because you have received what our friend Peter the Gnome calls "the codes of light." These are codes that you can, from that point forward, replicate inside each of your cells on your way to becoming a true knight of cosmic light—*Homo lightenoid*. From there, when you meditate, you can meditate on that for a few moments, because you have a cellular experience and now a memory of what water can be.

∽

ABUNDANCE BEGETS MORE ABUNDANCE

Modern mathematics teaches us that one plus one equals two. That is not an algebra based on *MANA*. The esoteric understanding in alchemical science is that when you get two together, all of a sudden you have three. Now here is where the principle of *MANA* (Ormus) really begins to deliver its promise that all power is within us. Ormus displays what we call a "getter phenomenon." This means that when Ormus is in high concentrations (in a person, location, object, rock, water, etc.), it can spontaneously get higher—the concentration of Ormus can instantly increase. Ormus is known, under certain conditions, to attract more of itself from out of the aethers (from another dimension). Simply being aware that Ormus exists and focusing on gathering more of it into yourself is often enough to feel some effects! This is especially true in places saturated with Ormus, such as Hawaii. In these places it is easier to draw the *MANA* into you.

As long as you live, *MANA* cannot be completely excreted, it cannot be totally lost; it is always there at some level in reserve. Muhammad Ali said, "I hated every moment of my training, but I knew if I just didn't quit, I'd live my life as a champion." He knew inside himself there was something more that was always in him, no matter how fierce the fight or how exhausting. Even when everything seemed to be gone, Ali knew that if he just kept going he would regain a second, third, fourth, or fifth wind—whatever was needed to win. The power he was able to draw upon is the hidden *MANA,* the eternal ocean of infinite energy.

NICK: "Ali," by the way, means *God's fearless warrior*. Muhammad Ali has inspired a lot of us. He certainly has inspired me. As a boy I would always get my Dad to wake me in the wee hours of the night to watch Ali's live fights. His "float like a butterfly, sting like a bee" mantra gave him a mystical shamanic power that his opponents did not possess. His poetry and mantras were personally empowering to him, so much so that he managed to define himself as a unique force in a very rich epoch. The quality and ability of his contemporaries during those years has never been surpassed; his was the Golden Age of heavyweight boxing and yet he stood atop the mountain on account of his abilities to tap resources that the other fellows could not access. I learned the principles he applied and tested them in the Thai boxing rings of Asia and Europe. They were so effective that within one year of experimentation I fought a former European light heavyweight kickboxing champion on three separate occasions.

I never fought because I was vicious or nasty or enjoyed hurting people, but it was the training ground within which I could confront fear and deal with inhibition in such a definite way. Fear is the great debilitating, constricting, contracting emotion. It is no coincidence that fear is the central component of the ego. Fear can constrict and distort the free-flow harmonic of *MANA*.

THE FORCE

"The Force is what gives a Jedi his power. It's an energy field created by all living things. It surrounds us and penetrates us. It binds the galaxy together."

—OBI WAN KENOBI, *STAR WARS*

In the *Star Wars* sagas powerful archetypal messages and images were delivered to millions of individuals all over the world.

At present, most individuals are functioning only through five defined sensory modalities—eyes, ears, nose, taste, touch—and they process sensory information entirely based on logic and reason and therefore are unable to feel The Force. The five senses comprehend less than 0.000000000000000000001% of the available cosmic energy spectrum. And even what is comprehended with them is then distorted as it goes through other neural, mental, and cerebral processors, which are all based entirely on past, often haphazard, programming.

The Force is a feeling experience. You can feel it physically, but our real relationship with it is in a mystical realm. The Force is the mysterious energy and information that comes out of the aether, through the Ormus elements, and into our reality.

In the *Star Wars* films, a mythic name was given for the Ormus elements. They are called midi-chlorians.[5] The midi-chlorians are actually conscious atoms inside different beings that are intertwined with The Force and, if you have a significant quantity of those, then you have the potential of becoming a Jedi knight (superhero) or a Sith Lord (Illuminati leader)—you have the potential of manipulating The Force.

As it relates to our subject matter, the Darth Vader (dark father) archetype is very special, because Darth Vader, as a child, had the most midi-chlorians ever discovered in any being. That's why the Jedi knights believed him to be the chosen one. And then, what happened was he got distorted, he got tweaked, he got turned into an industrial machine. He became a Sith Lord through a distortion of his consciousness using The Force.

The Force can take us either way; it can amplify either constructive goals or corrosive behaviors. This thin line continuously tempts the main character of the greatest story ever told, keeping us at the edge of our seats. This looming danger of turning to the dark side must be present. The Jedi superhero, at this juncture, reflects upon the training of the last chapter: *MAKIA* (energy flows where attention goes). Through *MAKIA,* the superhero stays on track.

As we develop a positive, constructive relationship with The Force, we get out of thinking and into feeling. We can feel so much more wonder in nature with our souls than we can see with our eyes. We can actually feel the vaulted beauty of nature, and we can truly "find tongues in trees, books in running brooks, sermons in stones, and good in everything." The line of spiritual inquiry that the superhero pursues is simply how to become aware of more than 0.000000000000000000001% of what actually is.

The superhero ethic does not reason and rationalize or believe in The Force. Those thoughtforms are actually traps played by the mind. Rather than belief, the real question is how do you *feel* about it? What are you feeling in your heart? How are you feeling right now? When you hear about a race somewhere on some other planet that actually blew up their planet, and then destroyed the next planet they tried to live on, and then finally became conscious, got out of conflict, all became Ascended Masters, and instead of being happy building pyramids and meditating in caves, built superships and traveled across the cosmos to see how big God really is and are sitting right at this very moment on the other side of Saturn's moon Titan, how does it make you feel? Inspired!? Astonished!? Excited!? Happy!? Imagine, an entire race of aliens that saved themselves from themselves and made it into high levels of enlightened consciousness—that is the true potential of The Force.

All that might be too much for our imagination, so we recommend using an application of The Force called the Jedi mind trick[6] while going through customs or security when you travel. The power of it is just an awareness. If you didn't know about the Jedi mind trick, you could not use it. We find that using your consciousness to influence reality directly while under pressure is always surprisingly effective.

◎◎

Consider This …

Two overweight sad people are sitting down to a dinner of microwaved pig with their two children. In the background, the TV is playing some mind-numbing and emotion-lowering nonsense.

Inside the minds of the children, something miraculous is happening. The walls of the house have been blown completely off. The front door swings open, and a gust of wind sweeps in. The ceiling disappears as the nighttime stars peer down. Images of adventure, starships, and a universe of infinite possibility pour forth.

Outside, a benevolent and all-giving universe. Inside, a microwaved pig.

Wafts of magical foods growing in sacred megalithic gardens strike the children's imagination. Images of beauty—mountains, streams, rivers, still lakes, quiet forests, and leaves—engulf the two young minds.

In thought, the children move out of the house, partaking of the natural delight. They transform, as if by magic, into supernatural beings. The atmosphere around them becomes magnetically charged with the dance and crackle of ions, Ormus, and bions. Enchantment is everywhere. With an intimate, living wisdom, the children turn to face the deep ancient forests knowing something has awoken.

☯☯

The Most Powerful Technique Ever for Becoming Saturated in Ormus

Superheroes (cosmic knights) tap into the Ormus through their genetic blueprint, which may act to attract Ormus elements in from the aethers. History and some study on the subject confirm that the predisposition for certain types of awarenesses and paranormal abilities (siddhis) are simply present in some individuals at birth. However, genetic fortune is not the entire picture.

Some individuals have done years and years of focused research on the proper air, food, and water to ingest and diets and exercises to do (raw food, herbs, superfoods, chi gong, yoga, dance, surfing, hiking in Nature, ujjayi breathing) in order to absorb the maximum amount of Ormus, *MANA,* prana out of the environment. Some have moved to areas rich in *MANA* in order to soak it in by simply living there. Others have sought how to remove blockages in order to allow *MANA* to flow in. These approaches are fantastic and produce measurable results, but this is not the entire picture.

Muhammad Ali said: "I said I was the greatest in the world, long before I was, and long before I believed it." His repeated mantra, "I'm the greatest," and the power of those words could elicit in Ali's psyche a spiritual fervor that allowed him to open mysterious soul powers and draw in the *MANA*. He attracted it. He cultivated the *MANA* inside himself. This is a very powerful concept. You can increase the amount of *MANA* in your body, by meditating on it. But first you must know the meditation and what "it" is.

The secret of *MANA*, the most powerful technique ever for drawing in Ormus, is meditating within, on, and around *inspiration*. Inspiration activates the Ormus light body, draws *MANA* in, and opens the floodgates, allowing in a universal abundance of energy and information. In the golden flow of inspiration, there is an infinite power. This is why "having the best day ever" is not optional—it is an Ormus-gathering technique. Something can come from nothing whenever you access that state. The Israelites were sustained by *manna* from heaven during their forty years in the wilderness. The Sanskrit word for this mystical nectar is *manmanabhav*—it is the golden juice of yogic communion, the most sublime and subtle, magical, and mystical element of our existence.

Living in a state of perpetual inspiration—where you can access what inspires you, where chills are constantly running up and down your body, where the entire mystery of the universe is perpetually intriguing you in the most fascinating journey of discovery ever, where you daily sip the nectar that transforms you, where you can take your rightful place in a starring role as the underdog in the most thrilling, heroic, unpredictable tale of love, mystery, suspense and triumph ever imagined—this is the true destiny of the cosmic superhero.

◎◎

ALEXANDER THE GREAT

More than 2,300 years ago, Alexander the Great led a forced march across a hot and desolate plain. On the eleventh day, he and the soldiers still with him were near death from thirst. Alexander took the lead and pressed on. At midday, two scouts brought him what little water they could find—it was just a few sips rolling at the bottom of a helmet. Their throats burning, Alexander's men stood back and watched him enviously. Alexander turned the helmet over and poured the water on the hot sand at his feet. Then he said, "It is of no use to drink when many thirst." The men desperately needed water, but they received instead something much more valuable, something Alexander alone had to give: inspiration.

NICK ON MANA

MANA gives us presence. Recall how at the beginning of this book we talked about the joyous fact upon which these principles are founded, that something wonderful exists inside us. Well, now we know it is inside everything. All around us. Everywhere. For me, the most amazing thing is the way our conscious intent magnetizes this magic through inspiration. As we invest our love in *MANA* we draw it into us and it activates our being. I love the way this is so alive. How relationship replaces theory. Feeling replaces idea. This is the metaphysical aspect of personal alchemy. And we can tap the *MANA* anytime.

Perhaps the simplest thing we can do is breathe it in. One person can be taking a breath unconsciously and the next person breathing consciously; the difference in what they absorb is the difference between being an immortal yogi superhero and an ordinary person. That's the difference. It is a great question to ask yourself: Where is my awareness?

"Your breath is tantamount to a continuous meeting between us, your angels, your higher consciousness, and your Earthly Self. It is a round-table discussion in which your next move is planned and then the next. All of this is based upon your intentions you see. With your out-breath we are able to extract from you that which you no longer desire and with your in-breath we imbue you

with positive direction, which holds you up in the face of appar-
ent discord."

—DOREEN VIRTUE, MESSAGES FROM ANGELS:
WHAT YOUR ANGELS WANT YOU TO KNOW

Imagine an Ormus-soaked biology: every cell in your body switched on,
happy, juicy, and saturated in Ormus. What would happen?

Thoughts of infinite love and wonder, fueled by feelings of compassion floating across consciousness. Super-healthy cellular structures resonating with the highest frequencies of Creation. Natural
substances of the highest order loaded with X-factor possibilities
increase the fluidity of being. As feelings of hope, compassion, and
appreciation move deeper into the soul, the feelings of love and gratitude and awareness of infinity crystallize—the confluence of these
factors activates a biological transmutation. In a divine metamorphosis what was an ordinary human being now becomes a supernatural being, a superhero, something that had been intended all along.

@/@

"I am the bread of life.
Your ancestors ate the manna in the desert, but they died;
This is the bread that comes down from heaven so that one
    may eat it and not die.
I am the living bread that came down from heaven;
Whoever eats this bread will live forever;
And the bread that I will give is my flesh for the life of the
    world."
The Jews quarreled among themselves, saying,
"How can this man give us (his) flesh to eat?"
Jesus said to them,
"Amen, amen, I say to you, unless you eat the flesh of the
    Son of Man
And drink his blood, you do not have life within you.

Whoever eats my flesh and drinks my blood has eternal life,
And I will raise him on the last day.
For my flesh is true food,
And my blood is true drink.
Whoever eats my flesh and drinks my blood remains in me
    and I in him.
Just as the living Father sent me
And I have life because of the Father
So also the one who feeds on me will have life because of me.
This is the bread that came down from heaven.
Unlike your ancestors who ate and still died,
Whoever eats this bread will attain everlasting life."
—JOHN 51-56

◎◎

4. MANAWA—*Now is the Moment of Power*

Now is the Moment of Power. Be Here.
Strike While the Iron is Hot.

The fourth Huna principle is *MANAWA*. If *MANA* is "all power comes from within," what do you suppose *MANAWA* means?

    What it means is: Now is the moment of power. Many people have read Eckhart Tolle's popular book called *The Power of Now*. Spiritual leaders all over the world seem to be copying each other by telling us from all directions "we've got to get into the moment," into the "now." We have heard "Be here now." Yet at this point we know there actually is truly no "now." Time is the eternal flow—the eternal flow of what is happening.

THE ETERNAL FLOW

The eternal flow is a useful concept because of the similarity to flowing water. The most incredible technologies await us as we begin our research into what water really is, how it flows, and what it wants. We will rediscover the levitational free-energy water and air technologies known to the Atlanteans by studying the great insights of the Austrian Water Wizard Victor Schauberger,[7] who gained his technological understanding from watching water flow.

Yet at this point, as we understand that time, like water, flows dynamically, we gain a unique perspective. The flow cannot be boxed up or dammed up; it cannot be compartmentalized. Time like water inrolls upon itself, swirls, forms eddies, curves, twists, and turns. And in the alchemical mixture of time's flow, the souls of the living are sediments carried for some time and then redeposited back upon the beaches of universal consciousness.

Basically, you could be in the flow of what's happening or you could be caught up in eddies (false identities) that can drag you into the depths, stagnate your soul in the muck, and finally dry out and crack. Your goal is to be carried in the very center of the flow for as long and as far as possible.

And what happens at the very center of the flow of the river? The flow organizes the water into active regions separated by thin lines of increasing coolness and oiliness—Ormus. The coolest section, that area most in the flow, flows the fastest. The water becomes levitated; it becomes happy. The excitement is high. Destiny comes into vision. Magic becomes palpable, normal laws break down, as the *MANA* swirls in.

Being in the flow means you must be flexible in order to stay with it. Flexibility is the first sign of youth. Rigidity or solidification of thought, word, or deed immediately sets one into the distracting eddy currents and beaches the soul.

Think about Muhammad Ali, who stayed in the flow by repeatedly using his code words, his mantra, that became as famous as the boxer himself. Everyone knew his mantra: it was "float like a butterfly and sting like a bee." And if you remember the way he used to move, unlike any other boxer that's ever trained, he could float around that ring. He was in the flow and therefore had a magical presence.

Being in the flow is not the occasional pastime of the superhero.

It is the daily meditation—the goal. How do you know if you are on track? Synchronicities, little clues from the aethers will tell you. And how do you keep manifesting synchronicities? By following the clues, watching the clues, and researching them like a detective. One must follow up on clue after clue until the surprising conclusions are reached, and then *those* must be acted upon. This is the essence of how the greatest story ever told actually evolves.

To evolve with the flow, one becomes a master of transformation. Never-ending change is a way of life in today's hyper-paced world. To stay one step ahead of the game we master change by accepting it and by embracing it with superhero consciousness.

⊚⊘

NICK: All my life I have been living my dreams, overcoming fears, and achieving consistently higher and more challenging goals. It all began on the cold and wind-swept rugby fields of England. As a boy I lacked physical toughness, self-confidence, and belief. I was not a fast runner. I had long skinny legs and not much skill. Rugby is a little like American football without the helmets and pads. The best players are tough, fast, and talented. I was consistently told all the way through my rugby career that I was not good enough. This did not stop me, and I went through school into men's teams winning major competitions, being the youngest player in the most senior teams, captaining my college team, representing my county at the provincial "under-23 level." I was part of a record-breaking season in one club's history of forty-seven games without defeat, and I was a top *try* scorer myself, while helping to make my wingers record-breaking *try* scorers. Sometimes I would play three full-contact games a week and train every night except Tuesday. I went on to play Senior First Division rugby in Auckland, New Zealand, the most ferocious competition on Earth. I also played in Sydney, Australia, and South Africa. The club I played for in Durban, South Africa, was unbeaten as well. I scored incredible, memorable tries, as the Durban team went on to win the

Currie cup and become the top team in the country.

It was not just on the rugby field that I overcame inhibitions and lack of ability to achieve. I did it in the boxing ring as well. As an unbeaten amateur boxer in New Zealand, I sparred with some of the best pros in the Southern Hemisphere, including Tony Mundine, the only Australian professional fighter never to be beaten by an Australian. Tony fought for several world titles and was a light heavyweight, heavyweight and middle-weight champion. I boxed him over three joyous rounds in Sydney one day after meeting him in a restaurant the night before. It was the day I was leaving Australia for South Africa. I went down to his gym in Redfern and had a most glorious tear-up. Boarding the plane to leave Sydney that same afternoon with a fat lip and sore ears, I felt on top of the world.

What I learned is that, in the middle of a bout or a game, a window opens for a fraction of a second, and if you're in the flow, you can bust through a gap. It's not a decision, it's an instinctive reaction that you witness as you do it. Observation and action become one. Being aware, like a fighter, like a hunter, invites advantageous experience in your life. But if you procrastinate, that window of opportunity will close, and it can snap shut in a fraction of a second. There are opportunities— magical, synchronistic, wondrous opportunities. It's all about being there for those moments . . . being in the flow.

☯☯

THE POWER OF NOW, REVISITED

So what of the "Power of Now"? The word "now" as defined by a common dictionary is like an irrational number—"now" is always defined in synonyms. There is no "now."

However, when we define "now" as the instant of a decision, then the concept becomes useful. Author and success lecturer Og Mandino's phrase "Do it now. Do it now. Do it now" suddenly becomes power-filled. *MANAWA* gains mystical levels because it indicates that the decision is the power.

Let's reflect on Og Mandino for a moment. This guy was a drunk, he was a bum, he was living on the streets, he had nothing left, he debated suicide, but something else happened instead. Here's his story . . .

One cold wintry morning in Cleveland, one I shall never forget, I almost took my life. I had passed the window of a dingy pawnshop and paused when I saw, inside on a shelf, a small handgun. Attached to its barrel was a yellow tag . . . $29. I reached into my pocket and removed three ten-dollar bills—all I had in the world and I thought: "There's the answer to all my problems. I'll buy that gun, get a couple of bullets, and take them back to that dingy room where I'm staying. Then I'll put the bullets in the gun, put the gun to my head . . . and pull the trigger. And I'll never have to face that miserable failure in the mirror again."

I don't know what happened next. I joke about it now and say that I was such a spineless individual at that time that I couldn't even muster enough courage to do away with myself. In any event, I didn't buy that gun. As the snow was falling I turned away from the pawnshop and commenced walking until I eventually found myself inside a public library. It was so warm after the outside chills of November.

Og Mandino made a decision—perhaps a subconscious one. He got away from the pawnshop by walking into a public library, and he started reading books on how to make something out of his life. If you go into any dark, cold, ugly industrial city in America, look for the light emanating from a quiet public library. It is there for you. And that library has all those books, all that literature, all the spells, everything you could possibly imagine to transform you from zero to superhero. Gems, jewels, and treasures unbound await you in every single library. And Og Mandino went from the thought of suicide as a drunk in the gutter all the way to being the number-one success speaker in the world and author of some of the most popular books ever published in the field of success and personal development. His mantra became: "do it now, do it now, do it now."

The most powerful actions may be generated by decisions inspired by simple catalysts that arise from the most basic ideas. And it's right here, the catalyst: Do it now. Right here with you always: Do it now, do it now, do it now, do it now.

When's the time? Now. What's the best time ever? Now. Going to do it later? No, later never arrives. Right now. Now is the time for action. How many times have we heard "I'm going to do that later"? No, do it now. Do it now. Do it now. The decision is made. It is done.

◎◎

DAVID: One of the greatest teachings I ever picked up was from a success book by Tom Hopkins that states his Golden 12 affirmation:

"I must do the most productive thing possible at every given moment."

That simple statement changed my life. Just one sentence. You never know, you can open up one page of a book, and that is it . . . BOOM! . . . nothing is ever the same. You watch one movie, *Star Wars,* and learn about the Jedi mind trick (using your consciousness under pressure to transform reality), and now everything is different. You can go to one seemingly innocuous raw-food weekend retreat, and all of a sudden you come out of there knowing that the highest level of health is possible for everyone. What has happened?

You are discovering the power of information. Knowledge and information represent condensed time, condensed experience, condensed distinctions providing clarity about decisions. A book can flip your karma, a movie can alter your destiny, an audio recording can activate your soul.

Knowledge and information are content inside our story. This isn't the greatest mathematical equation ever told. This is the greatest story ever told! Therefore it must have some darn good intriguing content.

◎◎

Some people are not into doing things now. They are into doing things later. Some are into smoking cannabis on the beach, wasting time, and doing nothing. They are totally in alignment with that reality at every level of their consciousness. Instead of decisively doing things now, they typically select *manana* (a lovely word that Jack Kerouac suggested means heaven). However, these people are not on the superhero track. It is time to dump them and join a more challenging crowd.

Link arms with those who are going to push you to the next level, who uplift your spirits every time they see you and you see them. Meet people who are bigger than you, think bigger, act bigger. By "bigger," we mean individuals of lofty consciousness, language, and achievements. Consider the thoughts that are inspired within you while in the presence of such individuals. But make sure they are "the real deal." As long as they astonish you with their commitment to love and dedicate their lives to the betterment of themselves and the salvation of the world from ignorance, then they are the real deal.

❦❦

Decisions mean risk. Risk, not security, is the guiding force of winners. Taking huge emotional risks has created the greatest romances. Taking huge financial risks has created every billionaire. Taking huge psychological risks has created every champion.

When you select a course, pay attention.

Recall the Trial-and-Success formula discussed under the Huna Principle of *MAKIA:*

1. Know your goals inside and out via review and rewriting. Record your visions. Develop, in writing, the action plans.
2. Take action. Self-discipline is the ability to make yourself do what you should do, when you should do it, whether you feel like it or not. Use your laser-beam focus.
3. Be aware if your actions are bringing you closer or farther away from your goals. Be an objective witness.
4. Be flexible. Enhance your approach until you get the results you're looking for. Learn from your mistakes and adjust your behavior accordingly.

☙☙

Redeem, Correct, Perfect.

MANAWA: Now is the moment of power. Now is the best time ever because it is the instant of a decision. Succeed in your mission. Draw up your plan and take massive action. In motions of action, procrastination disappears. Develop and nurture the habit of seizing the moment by making decisions based on feelings in your heart. Listen to the highest voice you can hear. Immerse yourself deep in the sacred heart of the eternal flow—the source of infinite inspirational power, the wellspring of *Amazing Grace*.

Follow synchronicities into the flow. The power of the eternal flow is capable of wiping our karma clean and activating the expression of an underlying, eternal program—our mission, our original song.

☙☙

5. KALA—*All Change Is Possible*

Remember the source of the Huna principles—they are drawn from the Hawaiian pre-warrior society, before the Tahitian chiefs came. The original inhabitants of Hawaii were living in a paradise according to the spiritual principles of Huna. We are reviving and redefining these principles to help guide us through the unpredictable waves of our uncertain future.

KALA is Huna principle number five—all change is possible. There are only eternal horizons in every and any direction. There is no final answer to anything. When there is no choice, there is always a choice. When there is no way, there is always a way.

> **"There is always a way if you are committed."**
> —ANTHONY ROBBINS

"All knowledge exists in the universe and is available to anyone
who seeks it with earnest desire."
—(ATTRIBUTED TO) WALTER RUSSELL

☯

WORMHOLES

"Path presupposes distance;
if He be near, no path needest thou at all.
Verily it maketh me smile to hear of a fish in water athirst."
—KABIR

As we have seen, singularities (black holes) are built into every atom,
every cell, every plant, every animal, every human, every alien, every
planet, every sun, every galaxy.

Each singularity is a sacred heart or a strange attractor—a wormhole. Wormholes are holes in the fabric of reality that penetrate into
other dimensions and realities. Wormholes are magical vortices of
highly infolded knowledge and cosmic imagination beyond our own
normal waking understanding. Essentially a wormhole is God's mind's
eye peeking in.

In the realm of the wormhole, all rational thinking and logic break
down. The wormhole is irrational.

In order to have a habitually rational reality, you must have an
irrational component filled with exceptions somewhere—that is the
wormhole or singularity.

Basically, wormholes are an intrinsic part of all matter and, in the
case of *MANA* (Ormus) the wormhole (atomic nucleus) is bigger than
in normal matter and more influential in creating irrational, synchronistic phenomena in this reality.

Wormholes indicate that, in spite of the rational and logical habits
of nature, anything can happen at any time. We can at any time open
our heart to the unknown—the infinite possibilities of existence. We
can at any time say yes to *KALA*—all change is possible. We live in an

"anything can happen" type of dream. You never can tell what is going to happen next. The future is uncertain. That's what makes living so much fun.

OPENING AND EXPANDING AWARENESS

Language illiteracy is not nearly as dangerous as cosmic illiteracy. If you know your place in the cosmos, at least as best as you can understand it at the fringes of your imagination, you have leverage, insight, awe, and mystery—choices and change become possible. If you don't know your place in the cosmos, you have bills, politics, boredom, and television to contend with.

Cosmic literacy is created by awareness.

Our point of view holds that awareness is a primary component of consciousness and of individual potential and opportunity. Therefore, opening and expanding awareness by all means necessary may be considered the highest of human pursuits.

The opening and flowering of awareness can happen slowly, quickly, spontaneously, immediately, anytime, anywhere.

Some practical philosophies, lifestyles, and practices that facilitate the opening and expansion of awareness include:

> innocent perception
> diverse reading
> expansive traveling
> dietary exploration
> plant shamanism
> yoga
> chi gong
> unique film viewing
> meditation
> contemplation
> birthing

parenting
multiple relationship styles
diverse athletic training
agricultural pursuits (gardening)
animal communication
gaining financial independence
studying particular subjects independently or through
    disciplined educational institutions
public speaking
and several more ...

SHAMANISM: EMISSARIES OF THE PLANT MIND

Traditionally, the individual who was most interested in and who accelerated furthest into the depths of awareness and self-transformation was the tribal shaman.

The world's oldest profession is not what we thought it was; the world's oldest profession is that of the shaman, medicine woman, *kahuna,* or witch doctor.

Historically and mythologically, the true shaman comes into being through a near-death or highly symbolic death experience. Upon returning from the edge, the shaman has seen into the depths of the abyss, lost the fear of death (and life), gained a connection with invisible spiritual realms, and has attained superhuman powers. Afterwards, s/he has access to unusual knowledge, wisdom, abilities, and healing skills.

The shaman has gained the understanding that the universe is made up of language, not atoms. Author and techno-shaman Terrence McKenna said: "I don't believe that the world is made of quarks or electromagnetic waves, or stars, or planets, or any of these things. I believe the world is made of language." Language is information or code. Thus the universe consists of code. The shaman realizes this and then goes to work to hack into the universe.

A key aspect to hacking the universe involves an internal transformation created by retelling a new, better story of one's personal history, capabilities, level of awareness, attitude, cellular identity, soul's purpose, physical appearance, ability to relate to others, sexuality, and destiny.

The shaman directs energy inward towards spiritual, emotional, and physical perfection and encourages the tribe to do the same. This orientation inward seems to go a long way towards solving outer crises *before* they manifest as pessimism, doubt, anger, greed, control, conflict, war, etc.

The shaman usually becomes particularly interested in healing plants and herbalism. This leads to explorations into herbal medicines and tribal diet reformation. From the novel habit of trying new herbs and medicines first on her/himself, the shaman becomes a good metabolizer of poisons.

The shaman tends towards spiritual pursuits, and therefore diets are selected that are predominantly plant-based and light. Because the food is less dense, more nourishment is required from subtler forces.

Because the shaman is often concerned with the hardcore religious experience—the deepest sources and urges of the life force—this may result in a specific exploration into the power plants that interface psychically with human consciousness when ingested. These plants contain hacking codes (entheogenic compounds or entheogens) that allow the shaman to peer into the wormholes of reality. The power plants include: Ayahuasca,[8] San Pedro, Peyote, Magic Mushrooms, Iboga, Cannabis (consumed raw), *Salvia divinorum* (consumed raw), etc.

To the shaman, alterations of consciousness and perspectives are a way of life. The traditional use of power plants flavors each season with meaning and excitement. They add wonder, making life even more mysterious and fascinating. Through communion with power plants, the shaman becomes an emissary of the plant mind. This may take the form of environmentalism, organic agriculture, tree planting, stewarding of sacred lands and/or reverence for herbs and plant-oriented nutrition. Biochemical enlightenment is a real phenomenon. The shamanic plant path brings the tribal goal into view: genuine love, laughter, happiness, and inspiration, all under the umbrella of paradise on Earth.

Peering into the wormholes of reality using power plants or other means allows each individual shaman to achieve a galactic alignment of their soul with all of creation, from the Source to galaxies to suns to planets to aliens to humans to technologies to animals to plants to Ormus minerals to nature spirits and every frequency before, after, and in between. An inner alignment of consciousness opens a portal leading towards *beauty* as a way of life—as a consistent, enhanced feeling.

◎◎

THE BACKSTER EFFECT

Reports of the Backster Effect conveyed plant consciousness to the minds and hearts of people throughout the world. Cleve Backster delivered proof of a truth that shamans have known since time began.

On one unassuming morning in February 1966, Cleve Backster made a scientific discovery that changed the history of biology forever. Backster was at that time an interrogation specialist who left the CIA to operate a New York school for training policemen in the techniques of using the polygraph or "lie detector" test. The polygraph measures electrical resistance of the human skin and can reveal emotional uncertainty about different questions, indicating tendencies towards truthful or false answers. However, on that fateful morning a new potential for this instrument came to light.

Just after watering an office plant, Backster was struck by a unique idea: Was it possible, by recording the increase in leaf-moisture content with the polygraph, to measure the rate at which water rose into the plant from the roots to the leaves? Backster attached two psycho-galvanic-reflex (PGR) electrodes on either side of the leaf of a *Dracaena massangeana* (a potted rubber plant) and balanced his instrument before watering the plant again. There was no notable reaction to this stimulus. That is when Backster decided to try what he called the "threat-to-well-being" principle, an established method for triggering emotional responses in people.

First, he dipped one of the office plant's leaves into a cup of hot coffee. According to the polygraph, the plant did not react.

Second, he decided to get a match and burn the leaf properly. At the instant of this decision, at 13 minutes and 55 seconds of chart time, there was a dramatic change in the PGR tracing pattern in the form of an abrupt and prolonged upward sweep of the recording pen. Backster stated: "I had not moved, or touched the plant, so the timing of the PGR pen activity suggested to me that the tracing might have been triggered by the mere thought of the harm I intended to inflict on the plant."

THE SHAMANIC JOURNEY UNLEASHED

"Professional priests and theologians avoid
the religious experience."
—TIMOTHY LEARY, *THE POLITICS OF ECSTASY*

"If hallucinogens [entheogens] function as interspecies chemical messengers, then the dynamic of the close relationship between primate and hallucinogenic [power] plant is one of information transfer from one species to the other. Where plant hallucinogens do not occur, such transfers of information take place with great slowness, but in the presence of hallucinogens a culture is quickly introduced to ever more novel information, sensory input, and behavior and thus is bootstrapped to higher and higher states of self-reflection."
—TERENCE MCKENNA, *FOOD OF THE GODS*

The relatively recent explosion of power plants and entheogenic (psychedelic) compounds into the consciousness of the world has transformed the planet. It has helped usher in the computer age, the Internet, the flowering of spirituality, the sexual revolution, empowerment of women, global movements for disarmament, the continued devaluation of materialism, environmentalism of all sorts, and more *feeling* for our planet. Unfortunately, it has also cast individual souls into madness, depression, irreconcilable vistas of thought, and irresponsibility.

Should the power plants be available to the public? Are psychedelic experiences to be had by you and me? Are everyday individuals capable of integrating such experiences?

The flip side to the expansion of awareness and the inflow of knowledge using power plants is the potential for danger. Many people are not completely in their bodies. Their nutrition and overall level of mental and emotional health do not supply an ample amount of "groundedness" to allow their soul to remain fully anchored. Therefore, the psychedelic experience may be rife with side effects of mental illness, abusiveness, erratic behavior, the inability to integrate the experiences (flashbacks), spirit possession, entity attachments, irresponsibility, etc.

However, to put things in context, the danger of alcohol is hundreds of times greater than the danger of all the power plants combined.

It has been estimated that 0.7% of the planet is drunk at any one time.

Alcohol (especially distilled alcohol, also known as hard liquor) is the most dangerous of recreational drugs. Alcohol exacerbates control issues in people. Alcohol inhibits proper judgment, creates erratic behavior, increases meat consumption, causes dehydration, elevates anger, clouds one from seeing the consequences of one's actions, and invites one to forget. Alcohol abuse seems to symbolize everything that is wrong with civilized humanity. On top of this, drunk driving is one of the Western world's leading killers.

The fear and smear of entheogens is mostly exaggerated due to ignorance. Smear campaigns against entheogens are not new. The Spanish were battling the indigenous Mexican culture over the same three entheogens that are commonly debated today: peyote (or its extracted crystal mescaline), magic mushrooms (or its extracted crystal psilocybin), and ololiuqui, otherwise known as morning glory seeds (or its extracted crystal LSA, one molecule different from LSD).

That altered states of consciousness are natural, that plant medicines may help us experience a deeper organic connection with life so that we may better come to know the true nature of our self through these experiences, is a fact well known to the Illuminati. This understanding is a driving force behind the entheogen smear campaign and the simultaneous production and distribution of the worst forms of psychoactive synthetic drugs. Chemical concoctions such as crystal meth and its amphetamine derivatives (such as Ice), cocaine, methadone, valium, prescription amphetamines, prescription antidepressants, and many, many other dangerous psychoactive compounds are specifically engineered substances which distort one's perception of oneself and the world around us. The toxic side effects of these drugs are extremely destructive, and their addictive component is usually maximal.

Probably one of the most ridiculous positions put forward by the establishment is that the legalization of drugs or entheogens will cause society to disintegrate. Yet what we find is that the food of civilization (nutrient deficient, genetically-modified fare) is causing people to disintegrate. The food of civilization causes people to become demineralized, disconnected, ungrounded, unhealthy, and thus susceptible to danger with entheogens. The dangerous food of civilization, of course, is perfectly legal; its production is government-subsidized.

"The strongest argument for the legalization of any drug is that society has been able to survive the legalization of alcohol. If we can tolerate the legal use of alcohol, what drug cannot be absorbed in the structure of society?"
—Terence McKenna, *Food of the Gods*

The Appropriate Use of Entheogens

The entheogens are powerful tools. They demand a price of admission. You have to pay to play. You also have to pray to play. In the hands of the right people, with the correct nutrition, a formal ceremony, the proper intent, and a shaman to lead the experience, power plants can be extraordinarily healing and useful.

With appropriate usage entheogens produce acute effects and only subtle or no side effects. In fact, the main side effects are more psychological than anything else. In the short term, entheogens can be catalysts to the development of the imagination. In the long term, entheogens create links between plant consciousness and the human world.

The primary role of the shaman in a shamanic plant ceremony is to protect and safely lead others through psychic/spiritual energies or journeys. Training and instruction by a wise shaman are recommended when exploring the power plants. One should look for the following characteristics in a shaman:

Patience
Humility
Wisdom
Loving dedication
Sensitivity to the senses
Imagination
An open heart
Extreme groundedness

Most important of all is groundedness. The shaman or witch doctor must be the most grounded, level-headed member of the tribe. As Kerouac wrote of his famous character Dean in *On the Road:* "And Dean talked, no one else talked. He gestured furiously, he leaned as far as me sometimes to make a point, sometimes he had no hands on the wheel and yet the car went straight as an arrow, not for once deviating from the white line in the middle of the road that unwound, kissing our left front tire." No matter what, that tire was hugging that white line. That is how the shaman must be in order to navigate exotic forms of consciousness. If you are not like that, then the shaman's path is not for you.

The last thing we need on the planet is more flakes. Even Ken

Kesey, with his wily crew of Merry Pranksters who pioneered the psychedelic bus concept in the 1960s, was sure that his crew were not spaced-out junkies—they were intensely competent. They had to be able to catch and run with the ball at any moment.

The indigenous shamans of Central and South America are not fools nor irresponsible clowns either. They are great mothers and fathers of humankind. The Earth has always been understood by these native herb doctors. They are as essential as jungles, deserts, and rocks to the health of the Earth. They know that the ego-maniac, unsettled, self-important, money-mad ambassadors of Western civilization are on a timer that is ticking. These shamans are currently conspiring with plant consciousness to help heal people, cities, and environmental catastrophes.

⊚⁄⊚

SET AND SETTING

Ram Dass and Timothy Leary pioneered the understanding that set (internal mood and state of feeling) and setting (location) are major factors that determine the effects of the shamanic experience. Additionally, the quality and energy surrounding the plant itself are primary factors that determine the effects of the shamanic experience.

TYPICAL QUALITIES OF POWER PLANTS

* They help reconnect individuals with nature (plants, animals, and geography)
* They help reconnect individuals with each other (opening of the heart)
* They can decrease appetite
* They help alleviate or soften disease conditions
* They help alleviate or soften chronic conditions
* They naturally help numb pain
* They can increase energy

- ❖ They can help confer immunity
- ❖ They can improve cognition
- ❖ They allow for creative self-reflection

Words Other Than Drug for Power Plants

- ❖ Entheogen
- ❖ Magic molecule
- ❖ Medicine
- ❖ Sacrament
- ❖ Dehallucinogen
- ❖ Truth serum
- ❖ Reality intensifier
- ❖ Heart opener
- ❖ De-fearing agent
- ❖ Sacred substance
- ❖ Food of the gods
- ❖ Adaptogen

☯️

Ormus and Entheogens

The connection between the Ormus elements and power plants and compounds is not understood, although preliminary research findings suggest that power plants grown with Ormus-rich substances (e.g. ocean water or ocean-grown plant composts) are more complete, healthy, and full of potential experience.

The United States' Criminal Justice Industry

If you are an entheogenic explorer who feels you can safely navigate the psychedelic space, we recommend that you remain careful to avoid America's criminal justice industry, as its goal is to deposit in prison those who expand their consciousness. Explorations of consciousness are recommended to take place in countries outside the United States of America.

At present more than two million people are in U.S. jails. Of these, it is estimated that 13% are in for violent crimes and 67% are in for "drug"-related crimes.

Of course we feel that the idea of illegal plants is completely ridiculous; yet this is all part of learning to love the darkest age of botanical genocide.

TECHNOLOGY AND ENTHEOGENS

We have met living masters and thus we do not believe that all the masters are dead. But it may be true that all the technological masters are dead. Technological masters are highly spiritual individuals who completely understand how to design, build, construct, and prototype environmentally beneficial technologies in the form of free-energy machines that run on water and air.

We believe that certain specific areas of mastery may only be learnable from certain power plants. Our experience has indicated that many of the answers to questions regarding technological data as they pertain to free-energy machines may be known by certain power plants. It is possible that these plants are the key to our eventual arrival in heaven (outer space).

By all accounts the power plants contain one or more masters (enlightened teachers) within them. Carlos Castaneda and the Toltec tradition called the presence of an intelligent master within a power plant an "ally."

ᴏ⁄ᴏ

TIME BENDS WITHOUT BENDING

Can time change without time changing? Consciousness clicks off a certain amount of impressions each second—let's say that normal waking consciousness clicks off about three hundred impressions per second. Under the influence of entheogens or other altered forms of consciousness, or when viewing the product of a high-speed camera, the impressions received by one's consciousness can increase to a thousand impressions per second and time will appear to slow down.

Ultimately, the amount and depth of impressions available to consciousness per second is infinite, but in order for us to make sense of reality, this infinity is reduced to a number that the human nervous system can handle and make sense of.

◎◎

AYAHUASCA

DAVID: Ayahuasca is an entheogenic beverage from the Amazon made as a boiled-down tea primarily from two plants, *Banisteriopsis caapi* and *Psychotria viridis*. The shamanic history of Ayahuasca is legendary, and its impact on Amazonian shamanism and now the world is profound. In recent years, this sacred brew has traveled out of the Amazon with various shamans and the Santo Daime church. The two Ayahuasca plants are now being grown in tropical regions all over the planet.

I first drank Ayahuasca in Amsterdam in the summer of 2001. I had just finished a lecture on raw-food nutrition to a small group of interested individuals in one of the local conference halls. One of the attendees mentioned to me that he was conducting an Ayahuasca ceremony in a loft nearby that evening and invited me and my companions to attend. We quickly agreed without realizing what we were really getting into.

I believe in the power of plant spirit medicine; it is one of the fundamental tenets of my nutrition and herbal profession. However, I had never felt the power of the plant spirits so strongly as that night of drinking Ayahuasca. The experience was overwhelming.

I had brought two companions with me. One companion, a young woman from Spain, quickly became ill after drinking the brew and chose not to drink any further. Soon she fell asleep. My other companion drank once with me and we both seemed only mildly affected by the beverage. We sat and talked for an hour or so in the corner of this rather large loft-space somewhere in the middle of Amsterdam.

There were other individuals participating, at least ten others, and then there was the shaman leading the ceremony and his female assistant.

Upon observing others on the first drink, we could clearly see that some of the individuals were being strongly, psychically altered by the brew, especially a beautiful young Italian woman who seemed to be so innocent. Ayahuasca performed an exorcism of some kind of spirit from her that night that was one of the more profound and shocking things I have ever witnessed.

During the period of our first drink, my companion was being rather offensive to others. I was a little annoyed by him and gradually began feeling that it was better to start going into silent meditation. He continued to talk, to disturb others, and to display rude behavior.

Once we imbibed our second drink, the intense visions that Ayahuasca delivers overcame all of my ego. My friend, who had become quite rude, went deeper and deeper into despair and eventually was humbled in what could only be described as a "dark night of the soul." I had to clean up after him and it was a rather "full-on" experience under the circumstances of my own level of entheogenic inebriation.

Since that first experience, I have drank Ayahuasca more than thirty times with various shamans throughout North America and in the Amazon. When used with positive intent, I have found Ayahuasca to be a tremendous ally, a spirit of pure love, interested in the delivery of humankind from fear, arrogance, and environmental degradation.

However, just like all other powerful medicines, it must be properly prepared, taken with the proper shaman, and with the appropriate intent. Ayahuasca opens up psychic portals that are usually beyond an untrained individual's ability to close. Ayahuasca is far too powerful a substance to be consuming recreationally.

Ayahuasca is a soul medicine that I believe is going to play a key role in the great drama of the ages that seems to be presenting itself in the form of the intensity of our spiritual, environmental, political, and economic crisis. I believe that Ayahuasca contains a vast library of information and knowledge that can be drawn upon to heal our relationship with ourselves and our planet.

At the moment, a primary reason for my continued use of Ayahuasca is that I am exploring the history of the human race through this visionary plant. I have learned from Ayahuasca and different shamans that it (the vine *Banisteriopsis caapi*) is not from the Amazon originally, but was brought to the Amazon from Africa during Atlantean times. The vine is from Egypt or an area of Africa now under the sea, or a formerly tropical region that is now a desert. This seems to explain the association in the Ayahuasca visionary state of Egyptian deities (more than any other pantheon), dark-skinned peoples, Atlantean technology, as well as the whole Santo Daime focus on the holy lands, saintly figures (Jesus and Mother Mary), and the Temple of Solomon.

I also enjoy what Ayahuasca has taught me about other plants. As a "divining" substance that helps elicit the spiritual powers of herbs, Ayahuasca is unrivaled. This is an area that I am sure will be of continued interest throughout the future.

Currently, consuming Ayahuasca with the Santo Daime church in the United States of America is legal.

๑๑

Entheogens awaken the ability to have hyper-sensory perception, and then later help us to remain connected to these sensory perceptions during our normal state of consciousness. Ayahuasca, San Pedro, Peyote, Iboga, Magic Mushrooms, Cannabis (when eaten raw or "chewed"), *Salvia divinorum* (when eaten raw or "chewed"), etc. open doors that you cannot see or feel otherwise. They therefore quickly help you find these doors without having to waste dozens of years in meditation or in contemplation. Like a good book, entheogens condense time.

Primarily, entheogens can be activators of heart-centered awareness. The shaman's advice is to use power plants, if necessary, to open the doors into the heart. Once these doors are open, you do not require the power plants anymore—an opening has occurred.

"Well, it has to do with the peyote being not simply a biological, mechanical, chemical effect but one of spiritual transformation. If you undergo a spiritual transformation and have not had preparation for it, you do not know how to evaluate what has happened to you, and you get the terrible experiences of a bad trip, as they used to call it with LSD. If you know where you are going, you won't have a bad trip."
—Joseph Campbell with Bill Moyers, *The Power of Myth*

"Pursuing the religious life today without using psychedelic drugs is like studying astronomy with the naked eye because that's how they did it in the first century AD, and besides, telescopes are unnatural."
—Timothy Leary, *The Politics of Ecstasy*

⊘⊘

"Today's heresy is tomorrow's orthodoxy."

Action

"Better active today than radioactive tomorrow."

Some of us have always had a very strong predilection or prejudice or leaning towards the idea that it's not just all spiritual—that we're incarnated in a physical body for a physical reason and we are here to take action. So we believe in taking action. And action speaks louder than words.

One of the reasons why entheogens and power plants are not for everybody is because the abuse of such substances can paralyze the very core of what it takes to succeed in life—the ability to take action.

Action is powerful in this world. Practice makes perfect. Disciplined efforts over time create results. Discipline immediately creates order out of chaos. The industrialist Andrew Carnegie put it this way: "Anything worth having is worth working for." Success speaker Jim Rohn says it this way: "Discipline weighs ounces. Regret weighs tons."

◎◎

"Through repetition, the magic is forced to rise."
—ALCHEMICAL PRINCIPLE

Mastery is achieved through repetition and practice. The master understands that doing a thing well is never trouble.

KALA is active. Awareness without action is not nearly as powerful as awareness with action. It is all about action. It is about setting goals. It is about taking the vision, whether it is plant-induced or otherwise, and going out into the world and doing something.

We believe in taking massive action. That's a prejudice that we have. Some people disagree and feel that it's all about being and that we must meditate in a cave and pray for the salvation of humanity. We don't buy that that is the goal for everyone. We believe in thought, word, *and deed.* Right now, there are yogis still meditating in high-altitude caves in the Himalaya. We're glad they are there, but we need more action because meanwhile, down here, we've got depleted uranium being used daily by the U.S. military, we've got Chernobyl, we're being sprayed with chemtrails, we've got all kinds of terrorism against innocent citizens being planned, developed, and executed by factions of our own "governments" that then have blamed, or will blame, the whole thing on someone far, far away. There are unbelievable levels of deception. Those yogis are still in that cave. They're still meditating, they're still upside-down in an inversion, and it's all good. They're doing the whole trip, right? They're still in lotus position, right now at this second. Is it enough?

The beautiful thing about action is that it fits you perfectly. Whatever your area of interest, immediately start taking even more action in that direction. For example, let's say you're an artist. Create more art, keep pumping it out full-on day and night, get fully into it, go all the way into it.

Our great Earth asks for action, not words. The time to act is now and the need is urgent, for the fate of our home planet hangs in the balance. In spite of the overwhelming environmental, political, social, and emotional challenges we face, we can still solve them all and eternally ennoble the destiny of the planet Earth and all its residents.

6. PONO—*Harmony/Effectiveness is a Measure of Truth*

An expert is recognized by the altar s/he builds.

There are mystical golden threads that connect our inner and outer worlds. We can follow each thread from the core of our being outward towards everything we have ever put our attention on. If these golden threads line up harmonically like a musical instrument, they may be played symphonically. Harmony is the measure. This is the goal of *PONO*.

Have you ever considered harmony as a measure of Truth?

Is it possible that Truth is a living phenomenon in Life—not static or fixed?

Is it possible that Truth evolves and changes?

◎◎

THE ALTAR WE BUILD

PONO informs us that if we are ready to commit consciously to the highest experience available to us, then attention to our altar is required.

How have you adorned your altar?

We build an altar within us. It is our place of intimacy, of inner speak, the realm of our innermost being where our core relationship with the Spirit of Life is defined. It is here at this altar that the vibrations of all our thoughts, words, and actions alchemically transform into a living mandala of feeling states.

How we are feeling moment to moment is our test.

In the simplest sense, it is by "feeling the best ever" that we discover if indeed we have adorned our altar with jewels and gems of consciousness.

Are you ready to feel the best ever all the time?

Are you ready to make the quantum jump into the wonderful superbeing that nature has designed for you? A being that is already programmed into your super-conscious mind?

The Normal Waking State

A number of years ago scientists from Stanford University were conducting studies on human DNA. During their research they were amazed to find that a staggering 98% of our genetic material has no known function in what is termed *the normal waking state*. The normal waking state is the psycho-emotional-physical state we experience when we are awake and acting "normally" (within the context of today's society). In other words, the body-mind-feeling state we experience as a consequence of the current system allows us to experience only 2% of who we actually are.

We equate the normal waking state with an energy level equivalent to the living dead.

The psycho-emotional prison of the normal waking state is a mental construct, a web of reinforced ideas based on inherited and programmed misconceptions of reality. Inaccurate and disharmonious awarenesses prevent the inflow of natural potential. This mental format also re-directs creative life force energies into unnatural forms so that thoughts, words, and actions continue to co-create an unnatural world system that keeps re-imprisoning individuals in their own reflected poor-quality ideas and feeling states. Some of the consequences of feeling trapped within this prison include depression, ill health, violence and/or boredom.

Because you are reading this right now, the universe is asking you to wake up from the normal waking state. The universe is requesting that you explore novel waking states—states of conscious that are richer in awareness. Your exposure to the matrix's programming must cease, because it continuously reprograms individuals into the normal waking state.

The matrix's programming is broken apart and a new altar is built by: turning off your television forever, stopping addictions to the "news," only studying books, videos, and audios that are at the cutting edge of information-consciousness, adding in superhero nutrition (organic raw foods, superfoods, herbs, and chocolate), yoga and chi gong, experiences in wild nature, sun gazing, drinking the best water ever, attracting innovative friends who stretch your imagination, living in perpetual positive thinking, having the best day ever, writing down your goals, and all the other aspects of transformation whispered about in this book.

To help jumpstart the collapse of the old programs and to simultaneously begin your superhero life in earnest, we recommend that you participate in our *Success Ultra Now Personal Optimization Program* (SUNPOP).

SUCCESS ULTRA NOW PERSONAL OPTIMIZATION PROGRAM

We have developed a superhero training program titled the *Success Ultra Now Personal Optimization Program* (SUNPOP). SUNPOP is a guided inner journey that takes place while you listen, visualize, and relax.

SUNPOP takes visualization to innovative vistas. The system is a distilled synthesis of the most potent reality creation systems yet developed. Some of our research into this project has been quite exciting. This research includes studying a top-secret military program called Project Superman. This program was initially an experiment to engineer the ultimate super soldier, a virtually indestructible human being. His name was Andy Pero. Things went very wrong. The disharmony and mal-intent of the program caused its collapse. Yet the technology discovered by Project Superman is still useful when applied with an appropriate harmonious intent, as we do in SUNPOP.

This guided inner journey has been specifically engineered to allow us consciously to expand our levels of awareness and vitality as well as help us escape the normal waking state. This program immediately puts us in alignment with our soul's purpose (thus dissolving mistaken identities).

SUNPOP takes into account the mountains of research into the human psyche demonstrating that our subconscious mind stores all the memories of every felt experience. The most impactful experiences the subconscious has witnessed are the ones that make the deepest impressions. Many of the negative behaviors we have expressed since childhood are based on judgmental reactions to emotional experiences. The wounded soul has a tendency to crystallize negative experiences into blockages within our energy meridian system. Judgmental reactions scar our consciousness with grooves that redirect our spiritual energy like a river that has been dammed through constructions of steel and concrete. As our spiritual energy flows into energetic dams, patterns of thought, feeling, and emotion often recreate emotional feelings we should have left behind long ago.

The behavior patterns which result as a consequence of judgmental reactions and energetic blockages have been defined by leading medical intuitive Dr. Carolyn Myss into four primary archetypal categories:

> The Wounded Child
> The Prostitute
> The Victim
> The Saboteur

These behavioral tendencies, and the underlying attitudes which drive them, are dysfunctional and produce negative emotional responses such as hate, shame, fear, guilt, anger and/or viciousness.

SUNPOP is specifically engineered to use the hidden power of forgiveness to identify and uproot any of the four behavioral tendencies that may be present within us. SUNPOP may be the most important exercise into personal forgiveness you ever undertake.

Additionally, SUNPOP takes us into mental, emotional, spiritual, and archetypal realms where gigantic, metaphysical forces interface with our soul. By utilizing the technology of SUNPOP, we can reconfigure how these metaphysical titanic forces interface with our soul.

As a result SUNPOP helps us become a more activated superhero— a living embodiment of the solution to the world's challenges. A great return to innocence, of which the prophets foretold, suddenly becomes possible.

The *Ormus factors* specifically activated by the SUNPOP guided inner journey include:

❖ Reconnection with Nature

❖ Peace

❖ Surrender

❖ Breath activation

❖ Ascension

❖ Sacred heart activation

❖ Illumination

❖ Forgiveness

❖ Gratitude

❖ Love

❖ Appreciation

❖ Patience

❖ Cosmic magic

❖ Vision

- ❖ Focus
- ❖ Harmony
- ❖ Color
- ❖ Courage
- ❖ Service through kindness

The goal of SUNPOP is to allow us to enter upon the trail of the blessed, cross the sacred valley where angels dwell, site distant noble goals, swim in the mighty river of beauty, release dammed-up emotional energy, and navigate into the holy flow.

For more information on SUNPOP or to begin the program immediately, please visit www.successultranow.com.

DAVID AND GOLIATH

"These times are the greatest of all times in your recorded history. Though they are difficult and challenging times, you choose to live here during this time for the purpose of your fulfillment."
—RAMTHA

It is upon the stage of life that we stand together in the greatest love story ever told. David takes on Goliath. The winner takes all.

Few stories are more relevant to our position in the current world situation than David and Goliath. In the classical Biblical tale—a metaphor for ascension—the young boy tending his goats on the hillside is watching the battlefield below, as the armies of Israel and the Philistines square off against each other. As was the custom in those days, the champions of each army would come out to fight before the battle began. Sometimes the battle was decided by a fight of the champions. According to The Bible, for forty days Goliath stepped forth and challenged the army of Israel to send out a champion.

This story is a metaphor. If we can tap into its spiritual meaning we can receive its hidden gifts of wisdom. In this story there is wisdom we can apply to defeat monstrous terrifying elements within our own psyche that may be preventing us from fully expressing ourselves.

Goliath was a giant and the champion of the Philistines. So imposing was his presence that none of the champions of Israel would fight him. This was astonishing to a teenage boy watching the scene. David was the youngest of four brothers who tended his father's sheep and goats. His three older brothers were all in the army of the Israelites serving under the king, Saul. One day, David's father Jesse asked David to take bread to his brothers on the battlefield. So incensed was this boy by the refusal of the soldiers to challenge Goliath that when he came down to the battlefield he demanded to fight Goliath himself. A meeting with the king followed. David was given armor to wear, which the boy tried then removed, owing to its heaviness. David understood his chance at victory would not be in one-on-one armored combat, but would rest upon his skill with his sling.

David carried no sword. On his way down to the scene of the battle, David picked five smooth stones from a running stream.

Goliath laughed and ridiculed the boy as David stepped forth into the arena of surrounding soldiers to face the giant.

Samuel 1:17 tells us that "the Philistine cursed David by his gods," but David replied: "This day the LORD will deliver you into my hand, and I will strike you down, and cut off your head; and I will give the dead bodies of the host of the Philistines this day to the birds of the air and to the wild beasts of the earth; that all the earth may know that there is a God in Israel, and that all this assembly may know that Yahweh saves not with sword and spear; for the battle is Yahweh's, and he will give you into our hand."

The story reaches its thrilling climax as Goliath begins to approach. At this moment David "runs towards" Goliath and, confident and unwavering, places a smooth, medium-sized river stone into his sling.

David swung and in expert fashion released the river stone on a mighty trajectory that shook the entire world. David struck the giant between the eyes before he could react. Goliath fell (directly) dead to the Earth. David leapt forth, then took Goliath's sword and removed the giant's head from his body.

On seeing their champion defeated, the hordes of Philistines turned and ran, and the army of Israel pursued them and slaughtered them right back to Gath. David went on to become Israel's most adored king.

Every aspect of the story represents something to us. The armies (on both sides) are representatives of materialism, greed, ignorance, lust for power, and fear. Goliath represents the oppressive material world. Among the two sides facing each other, no champion of God can be found—until David steps forth. The meeting with the king is symbolic of the world's education. The armor is a metaphor for the emotional armor worn by the ego—the false king. Our boy David has to try it on and then make a conscious decision not to wear it. Ultimately, David embodies the eternally youthful soul of possibility.

An aware reader's ears should prick up now.

NICK: A great message is being communicated in this tale and one which we consider central to the whole theme of this book. *Amazing Grace* is exactly that. The X-factor is the ingredient in the equation that allows us to defeat our "enemy" against all odds. This enemy is all of the negative programming of the world, all the orcs and goblins causing havoc within the human consciousness, all the false unnatural conditioning that pollutes the human psyche with so much toxicity that most of us are functioning on a tiny fraction of our available human potential and witnessing a world that reflects that toxicity. Everything we perceive outside ourselves is a reflection of the inner human environment. How do we remove this monster? Courage is one requisite factor. David had courage. The power of God's light illuminated David's inner world. David was also a child of Nature, he was still in touch with "the living God" directly. His power was not born out of a theory or concept, but from direct experience of real living qualities in the natural realm.

And what of the five stones, what are they? What are the five qualities we need to possess if we are to defeat the enemy within? David demonstrated:

❖ Courage

❖ Innocent perception

❖ Intuition and the ability to follow it and express it creatively

❖ A well-developed relationship with Life/God

❖ An unshakable conviction

Above all, David's unshakable confidence was founded upon one thing: his certainty of who he was as a child of the living God.

The story also asks us: Where are you in this tale? Are you, now, at this very moment, standing in the ranks of the Philistines, confident behind Goliath? If you are, the story is saying you're in for a big surprise. And that is what we are saying too.

You may have noticed that there is a David within you who is now hearing a call—an entirely surprising destiny is beginning to reveal itself.

The power to defeat Goliath is within our own psyches as it was within David's. That power is a power of certainty. The champion inside us is activated by certainty.

In Raja Yoga, we can all be the number-one jewel on God's diamond necklace of souls. The same thing is true in our book. We can all be David. The story of the ascending boy king, the *puer aeternus* of the present age, is the parable of the superhero.

In David's story it was literally a sling that served as his weapon of consciousness. For all of us this is just a metaphor—each of us possesses our own sling, the weapon of our mission on Earth. *PONO* indicates that effectiveness is the measure. What is the most effective weapon of consciousness you possess?

Now, in this human drama where Goliath is falling, we have a magnificent opportunity to step into the greatest flow ever. Our mythology is literally pouring like lava into a benevolent cosmic and divine ocean of opportunity forming zeolite molecules to cleanse and detoxify our planet, ourselves. At this incredible moment we have a remarkable choice to make. To cascade through as David and slay the Goliath of Illuminati Oz power, material greed, ignorance, arrogance, military industrialism, pharmaceutical disinformation, mega consumption, suicide ego-tripping mania **OR** to do what?

The "free-will experiment" decrees that a conscious choice can always be made. The choice is all about where we position ourselves on "the field." Being there is required. Whether through our attitude and awareness, we select the path of the ascending hero, a member of Goliath's army, or some other player in the drama is entirely up to each of us.

The future world is being generated right now. Like the greatest epic films, the hero/heroine will, against all odds, save the day, even at the last possible second. Our challenge to you is: *are you ready to play your part in the greatest story that has ever been told?*

Someone once said that life is not a dress rehearsal. Perhaps you have been living behind a curtain. Well, it's time to come out. What you have been hiding behind has dissolved before you. The heroism that is required in the times we share is heroism of the highest degree and calling.

THE SINGLE MOST CRITICAL FACTOR IN THE HEALING PROCESS

PONO instructs that the quest for harmony is the quest for truth and vice versa. The creation of harmonious feelings seems to occur consistently only when one is aligned in thought, word, and deed with one's life mission. Experience has taught us that *the single most critical factor in the healing process is the identification with one's true self and mission in life and then taking action in alignment with that mission.*

Harmony allows an ever-present power of natural magic to flow in. We function best in a state of harmony—in tune with the infinite. We flow best inside its cool hidden streams in peaceful tranquility.

Are you in harmony with life? Is it possible that the way towards your mission in life is a way forward that feels harmonious? Are you manifesting vibrant health and abundance in your life? What is the feedback life is giving you about the levels of harmony you are consistently demonstrating? What does your investment portfolio of feeling states look like now?

Fulfillment comes from doing one's mission—being true to that holy calling.

As you get more into your mission, your mission gets more into you. The mission evolves. It takes twists and turns, keeping you on your toes at all times. Be sure to evolve with your mission. This is the nature of your Jedi directive.

No matter what we witness in these times ahead, no matter how dreadful the evil, we must keep our innate sense of knowing and acting upon our mission. By all indications, this is our guide, our path to God.

We suspect that your mission brings a gift of kindness to the world. This is the natural by-product of being a superhero.

By expressing our Truth, by becoming the mission we were born to live, we create Heaven on Earth.

What is your purpose for living?

What is your mission in life? Answer it right now in your journal or right here on this page. Act now. It is time to finally get on with the joyful mission of building an altar into the eons.

PONO HARMONICS

> The boar may run from the tiger, yet each is armed
> with deadly weapons. Usually avoiding a conflict
> is the most harmonious choice.

PONO gives us insight. It reveals before the light of Truth that our thoughts, words, and actions constantly strike chords upon ever-present hidden metaphysical musical instruments, and it is the degree of harmony produced that defines the types of feelings we experience moment to moment.

By living from the heart in a constant state of simple adoration and awe of the infinite wonder of life and then acting in alignment with our mission as we build success upon success and construct an altar of achievement, we automatically play harmonic chords into our biology and the nano-consciousness that fills every cell. Indeed cellular structure is 98% consciousness (empty space) or what quantum physics calls *a unified field of infinite possibility*. Like a fertile garden of wonder, the soil of imagination that permeates our cellular structure responds to the thoughts, feelings, and actions that are constantly being seeded every moment of every day by every single one of us. It is in our own imagination about ourselves that the great miracles of the future will be discovered.

Consider this: we are living in unprecedented times. The debris that this civilization leaves behind will be here on Earth forever. Nothing like this has ever happened before. The imminent challenges that we face collectively and individually are of titanic proportions. The unsinkable present-day "scientific" civilization has already hit the iceberg and now we stand together. In discord and confusion, some are wondering who will make it on the lifeboats. In perfect harmony, the superhero wonders when Tan and crew are swinging in on their whisper crafts for a last-second pick-up.

7. ALOHA—*To Love is to Share the Happiness of the Breath of Life*

And now we move into the seventh principle of Huna, which is Hawaii's most famous word. What is the one word everybody knows from Hawaii? *ALOHA*.

ALOHA is the pure joy and happiness that emanates from just being alive. It is the joy of existence. It is an attitude of gratitude. It is the appreciation of beauty. *ALOHA* represents everything that is good and right in the world.

ALOHA is what you feel when you step off that plane that just landed in Hawaii. It is that greeting, that sharing of the breath of life, that magic, that feeling that it is good to be alive.

The exuberant joy of living—that is the *ALOHA* spirit.

"OTHERS"

As stated, *ALOHA* means "to love is to share the happiness of the breath of life." The key word here is "sharing."

In order for positive action to occur—as called for by *KALA* (all change is possible)—*others* must become involved. The Salvation Army was founded on one word: *others.*

The powers we access through the Huna teachings can improve the state of our lives. Yet even more importantly, as demonstrated by Dr. Len and his Ho'o Ponopono practice (see the upcoming principle number nine) these Huna teachings can help heal others. Their power is amplified several times over when we focus our attention on helping others.

The following story is from Portugal, from a small town made famous by supernatural events in the form of reported and documented miracles of healing. For many years, devotees of the Roman Catholic religious groups throughout the world have traveled in pilgrimages to Fatima, Portugal, because of reported visions of the Virgin Mary there by three shepherd children between May and October of 1917. They had this experience on the thirteenth day of each month at approximately the same hour. One of the children described seeing Mary as "more brilliant than the sun, shedding rays of light clearer and stronger than a crystal glass filled with the most sparkling water and pierced by the burning rays of the sun."

In the old quarters of Europe, a strong devotion to the Blessed Virgin led to the construction of a gigantic basilica built in honor of her aspect as Mother Mary in tiny Fatima.

Tens of thousands travel every year on pilgrimages to Fatima; often Mother Mary appears in visions and apparitions. Amazing, miraculous healings occur. The power of *Grace* is palpable. It is all well documented and fairly well known. Every disease, every human condition, every type of despair has been healed there. Yet not everyone receives the healing. Even receiving a vision does not ensure a healing.

Many years ago, Nobel Prize winner Dr. Alexis Carrell, curious about these healings and their apparently random nature, conducted a study to try and determine why some people were being healed and others were not. We may remember that Dr. Carrell became world-famous for proving that the cell, when properly nourished and cleansed, is essentially immortal.

Anxious to discover the common denominator shared by everyone had who received a healing, Dr. Carrell questioned each person, and he found that there was only one thing they all held in common. That one commonality was that they were all praying for someone else when they received their healing. [9]

The message is interesting. Focusing on helping *others* is the path towards miracles.

Joseph Campbell described a hero as someone who has given her or his life to something bigger than oneself. Getting addicted to a message bigger than oneself necessarily means helping *others*. It appears that when one starts thinking primarily about *others* and their ennoblement, then the door opens for heroic transformations of consciousness.

RELATIONSHIPS

As mentioned in *KALA,* we maintain a strong leaning towards the idea that just *being* is not enough. In order to really manifest a quantum and global transformation there's this thing called *relationships.* Relationships are as simple as one person communicating with another or one person communicating with a plant or one person communicating with their dog, etc. In quantum theory, relationships are simply event horizons (realities) bumping up against one another. No one is an island. Everything affects everything else. Relationships are intrinsic to every part of reality. It is really relationships that cause us to change and grow the most.

Remember the old adage that success depends on who you know, not just what you know. And it is not just who you know, it is who knows you.

There is no way we can activate our full potential with only ourselves. It is not possible. We can massage our own shoulders, but it doesn't feel that good. Try it right now. Massage your own shoulders. How good does that feel compared to letting somebody else do it?

What power is in our little fingers that makes others feel so good due to our touch?

Relationships, when channeled through heart-centered awareness, can cause us to develop excellent communication skills, beautiful emotional connections, deep loving feelings, appreciation for other points of view, and overall love for humanity and the human condition. In effect, relationships can lead us to the highest sensations of being alive.

The awareness that *KALA* has provided us is that all change is possible. When combined with *ALOHA,* we discover that all change is possible through the beautification, expansion, and deepening of relationships.

Relationships build families, teams, communities, cultures, and inevitably decide the fate of the world.

It is only by connecting with people through the power of relationships that one can be the individual who steers the slave ship and all of a sudden, at the last possible second, saves all from imminent destruction.

It all comes down to relationships and not just loving and productive relationships with other people, but also with animals, plants, water, air, fire, with our Earth, and especially with the Mystery. Ultimately, radically deepening our relationship with the Mystery—all the mysteries of existence—is going to be the key to creating paradise on our planet because it is the Mystery that can keep us forever enthralled, inspired, and happy to be alive without having to distract ourselves with conflict.

◎◎

THE MYSTERY

"The most beautiful emotion we can experience is the mystical. It is the power of true art and science. He to whom this emotion is a stranger, who can no longer wonder and stand rapt in awe, is as good as dead. To know that what is impenetrable to us really exists, manifesting itself as the highest wisdom and the most radiant beauty, which our dull faculties can comprehend only in their most primitive forms—this knowledge, this feeling, is at the center of true religiousness."

—ALBERT EINSTEIN, *HIS LIFE AND TIMES*

෨෨

WHAT IS YOUR RELATIONSHIP WITH THE MYSTERY?

Every human has a deep desire for certainty. This seems clear. People generally want predictability, schedules, and an assurance that things will continue on as before with some incremental improvements. However, an equally (if not greater) desire within the human psyche is the desire for uncertainty—the desire for the unfamiliar, the unknown, the paranormal, the startling surprise. These are archetypal elements intrinsic to any story; they must be there for the story of life to be entertaining.

For these authors, the proof of infinite intelligence woven into the depth of every conceivable thing is found in the fact that the more one researches a thing, the more one realizes how little is known about that or any other subject. The great historian Will Durant accurately wrote: "As we acquire knowledge, things do not become more comprehensible, but more mysterious."

An old adage reads: "I have been studying for so long that pretty soon I'll know everything about nothing or nothing about everything."

෨෨

MODIFIED ATMOSPHERES

ALOHA means: "To love is to share the happiness of the breath of life." Working backwards from "with" we discover *ALOHA* has much to do with the "breath of life." We view the breath of life as the essence of the mystery of life. The breath of life is completely intriguing in both a literal and metaphysical sense.

Why is it that the human organism modifies its atmosphere (e.g. smoking, air conditioning, humidifiers, etc.)? Why the connection between smoking (atmosphere modification) and shamanism? We suspect that the portion of our genetics that comes from the stars has great adaptability to modified atmospheres due to millennia of space travel. (This may also explain our tendency towards modifying our food.)

Why the presence of the root word "spiral" in respiration, inspiration, spirit, expire? The in-breath and out-breath of Brahma appears to be of a spiral character. Spiral action tends to increase the quality of the medium acted upon. For example, spinning water in a vortex increases its organization, improves its quality and taste, and subtly cools the water as well. The presence of spiral action in all living organisms indicates that the mere presence of life improves the quality of every medium life acts upon (e.g. water, air, soil, etc.). From this we understand that the second law of thermodynamics is incorrect—entropy does not rule, ectropy (organizational force) does. Quality (growth and information) continues to increase in our spiral galaxy. In general, this means that everything always improves and becomes more complex. Therefore, the Mystery continues to grow as the galaxy breathes (evolves).

◉◉

Shamanism, as described in *KALA,* is the original and still preferred practice and profession of perpetually opening to the Mystery. The opening of oneself to an experience of the Mystery is where spirituality begins and where materialism ends. Joseph Campbell wrote: "An intense experience of mystery is what one has to regard as the ultimate religious experience."

It appears that wisdom begins when one understands that the overall depth of the Mystery of life can never be known. Newer vistas of knowledge and insight always await.

◉◉

"The time will come when diligent research over long periods will bring to light things which now lie hidden.... Many discoveries are reserved for ages still to come, when memories of us will have been effaced. Our universe is a sorry little affair unless it has something for every age to investigate. Nature does not reveal her mysteries once and for all."

—SENECA, *NATURAL QUESTIONS*, BOOK 7, FIRST CENTURY AD

Consider the thoughtful words of mycologist Gary Samuels after his encounter with an unknown primate in Guyana (South America) in 1987: "I am not inclined to reveal just where I was when I saw this animal," he said, "because to be quite truthful, I do not want anybody to kill-stuff-study-catalogue it. It is possible that I saw nothing more than a spider monkey, but I do not think so. It is not important to me whether what I saw is confirmed to be something unusual—or usual. What I saw was outside my experience and that is enough for me. I rather like the possibility that there is some living creature, some primate, that has eluded Man. I like the mystery. It is important for me to know that there is such a mystery that might never be solved."

ALCHEMICAL IMAGINATION

The depth and awe of the Mystery can be felt at any time in the power of our imagination.

Our imagination is the great wonder of our species. All true transformation occurs first in the realm of the imagination. Every invention and creative contribution has first been a vision of imaginative dreaming. The grandeur of our imagination expresses itself most fruitfully in the high wonder and spirit of elevating *ALOHA* consciousness.

Our imagination is the ideal field of activity to lead us back to paradise and a truer understanding of the dynamic beauty and science of reality. Our imagination is our vision. It defines our feeling experience, our organic interface with matter, Ormus, *MANA*, and elementals mixed with soul. And imagination is always available to you each and every moment of your entire life.

Einstein worked out his Theory of Relativity by imagining himself careening around the universe on a photon of light. That is what he was doing in those pictures, that is why his hair was white and wild. He was not actually there in front of a blackboard writing with chalk all over the place in a dusty old room. He was out in the cosmos having a blast, exploring the fringes of his imagination.

Einstein said the following: "I am enough of an artist to draw freely upon my imagination. Imagination is more important than knowledge. Knowledge is limited. Imagination encircles the world."

The great writer, William Blake conjectured: "To the eyes of the man of imagination, nature is imagination itself."

Let's use our alchemical imagination for a moment . . .

Imagine ancient North America, where at one time regions teemed with mammoths, rhinos, camels, ground sloths, huge prehistoric bison, horses, and saber-toothed cats! Imagine our injured Earth repopulated by the beauty of these great animals.

Imagine every region of our Earth recognized for being holy and sacred. Picture ancient trees, mighty rivers, and lofty high mountains as temples of great power, held by people in reverence and awe.

Imagine homes built entirely of natural and recycled materials and filled with scents of wood, beeswax, and traces of burnt white sage, original paintings, marble sculptures, flow-form fountains, ergonomic furniture, natural lighting, and raw-food-based super-kitchens with a central giant wood-topped cutting-board island. Surrounding the home are gardens, unlike any ever seen before, that are rooted in well-loved soil loaded with Ormus concentrates. Envision flowers in profusion everywhere interspersed amongst the berry bushes, fruit trees, and magnificent beds of vegetables. Hear the sounds of children playing in nearby tree houses having the best day ever!

Picture in your mind's eye regions underneath the earth, where there are hidden caves of the cleanest water that moves rhythmically with the Earth's spinning motion. These aquifers are the veins of the Earth. Recall the mighty rivers that flow above the ground. These are the arteries. The oceans are the cellular fluid of the Gaian organism.

The land is the skin. The trees are the lungs. Imagine the mountains are the breasts. The high-mountain springs are the milk—offerings of pure love. The sun is the heart. The clouds are the thoughts of the Earth. Imagine that each rain is an insemination into the earth, and this, in conjunction with the female *MANA* in the Earth, produces life and sprouts seeds.

"The alchemists detect in the sexual activity of man a correspondence with the world's creation, with the growth of plants, and with mineral formations. When they see the union of rain and earth, they see it in an erotic sense, as copulation. And this extends to all natural realms of matter. For they can picture love affairs of chemicals and stars, a romance of stones, or the fertility of fire."
—Jim Morrison, *The Lords and the New Creatures*

"So we can say that hermetism and the Alchemical initiation are not related to modern chemistry by evolution or progress, but quite on the contrary, by degeneration. In this, as in other fields, modern science is built on the remains of ancient sciences, which have been gutted of their substance and abandoned by the ignorant and profane."
—Julius Evola, *The Hermetic Tradition*

Alchemy is an imaginative science; it is not just an intellectual understanding. Our ancient ancestors not only had a different way of thinking and feeling, but a different way of *perceiving* and *knowing.* They had a different technology, mathematics, and science; and they, like Einstein, used their imagination creatively to navigate these fields of knowledge.

Alchemy is, in truth, a natural science arrived at by applying the power of the imagination to grounded, observable and experimental phenomena found in nature.

We believe in the grand philosophy of the alchemists, namely, that the models to emulate are found in nature. Nature gently supports the imaginative *artist* who has been given insight into her operating system and perfects, in her domain, a creative project of some sort. An alchemical adage states: "The progress of the work pleases nature greatly *(operis processio multum naturae placet).*"

UNDERSTANDING EARTH, AIR, FIRE, WATER

The ordinary person does not know the four elements—Earth, Air, Fire, Water—*as they actually are in themselves.* Each person typically has only the ability to perceive what these elements are when they are intermixed with each other, not in their pure state.

Earth, Air, Fire, and Water as most people know them (that is, in their mixed state) are no more than reflections, or subtly tangible symbols, of the pure elements called "living" by the great alchemists. In themselves, the sacred four elements are organisms that possess great consciousness. Through alchemical and shamanic *imagination,* experimentation, and contemplation upon the four grand elements, one begins to penetrate into the consciousness of the pure elemental state.

For example, seeing, hearing, feeling, tasting, smelling and, in general, communing with Water in its purest, healthiest, ice-cold (39.2 degrees Fahrenheit or 4 degrees Celsius) state under moonlight as it freshly gushes forth from hidden springs filled with oily *MANA* in a pristine forest, makes one aware—through momentary glimpses—of how ennobled the consciousness of pure Water actually is. From such communions with the spirit of Water one can learn how to technologically endow water with what it requires to achieve the highest states of love and beauty while creating motive (motor) energy. In other words, by understanding what Water is and what it wants, one can develop free-energy technology that actually improves the fuel as it is used (in this case the fuel is water).

◎◎

To review, *ALOHA* means: "To love is to share the happiness of the breath of life." Working backwards from the previously discussed "... breath of life" we discover that *ALOHA* has much to do with "love," "sharing," and "happiness." The *ALOHA* spirit completely captures the essence of these three words. The *ALOHA* spirit is an attitude that knows we are supposed to be having the best day ever, every day. It includes a feeling of comfort with the great Mystery. It is an experience of feeling and knowing that all is good, and it is getting better all the time.

You might try switching from the word "Hello" and start using *ALOHA* instead. At first it may sound a bit strange, but after you get used to it, you won't notice it. People might think you are just back from Hawaii. Pretty soon, you might even find that your mom calls you up and says, "*ALOHA*." What happened? You are sharing the happiness of the breath of life.

PRINCIPLE NUMBER NINE: FORGIVENESS

"Mercy is the flower of growth."
—JESUS, *LOVE WITHOUT END: JESUS SPEAKS*

The great clarion call of The Ages is sounding out. You are being called, we are being called, we are ALL being called. Now IS the hour. The "bat-phone" is ringing. Our response to this critical call is absolutely defining human destiny. Of this there can be no doubt.

In Hindu mythology, on the battlefield at Kurukshetra, Krishna (the representative of divine presence) tells the weeping, unwilling Arjuna (the representative of the mind) that *he must indeed fight,* there is no choice. Essentially, Krishna informs Arjuna that action on the battlefield is required.

This is the time of radical action.

The archetypal fallen angels, writhing in their torment, have suffered enough. The sad tears of human history have scorched acid into the disguise our wayward people have donned.

The horrifying message of all pain, all war, hatred, violence and contempt, all bitterness, every rape, murder, abused child, pollution, disease, and absolute disrespect for all that is sacred is now communicated so loudly that even the ignorant beast that is present-day humanity is becoming restless and beginning to dream another dream—an entirely new way of life approaches.

As we steadily, one by one, little by little, together, open our eyes, minds, and hearts and miraculously, magnificently undo the shackles of insanity, we step out of the prison of judgment because we have found, hidden deep within us ... the key.

The key is forgiveness.

THE SPIRITUAL POWER OF FORGIVENESS

The most potent awareness catalyzing the activation of the super-hero—consciously adjusting the internal coding sequences to line up with synchronicities—is a spiritual attitude of forgiveness.

Forgiveness is a fundamental step into one's own true, innate, everlasting, all conquering, all healing, totally loving, eternally peaceful brilliance. Forgiveness is an endless spring of unknown prosperity. By embodying the attitude of forgiveness, we are released from our bondage—and all imagined bondage—forever.

Forgiveness is not an easy word for many; yet without it we do not possess the key to any prison cell. Forgiveness loosens the bonds of mental slavery and frees our heart.

Forgiveness opens the floodgates, allowing the *MANA* to flow in. Its power is felt immediately.

The opening of the inner flower of forgiveness—the Ormus moment—appears to be efficiently accessed when one is in direct communication with the one who is being forgiven. In this moment we are in reverence, at one, and in the solitude of wonder. In this moment we may receive the priceless gift of serenity.

As we apply forgiveness through our attitude and actions something significant occurs—judgment falls away, knowing disappears, and an opening to the mystery occurs. This happening is like Sir Percival acquiring the Holy Grail. Within the internal dynamics of this human interface with the Divine there is a subtle realm of an exquisite feeling experience rarely visited by heavy materialists. The purity required to discover the Holy Grail is simply the ability to let go of any grudges and forgive completely at all levels of feeling, awareness, attitude, consciousness, mind, and biology.

JESUS CHRIST SUPERHERO

In the example of Jesus Christ, his life and teachings, miracles of healing, crucifixion and ascension, the subtle, mystical, and all-powerful seeds of the almighty power of forgiveness were written eternally into the story of humankind.

Often referred to as the Lamb of God, Jesus (Yeshua) embodied qualities of being through an absolute awareness of Divinity and his relationship with it. His attitude of compassion with a core consciousness of forgiveness combined with his lamb-like innocence to create a clear illustration of the optimal state by which it becomes possible to access the *Amazing Grace* that empowers us all to perform the seemingly miraculous.

Jesus Christ's journey through brutality, through gore, through horror into heaven on Earth was activated through forgiveness—his last act.

In our opinion Jesus is one of the key superheroes in our recorded history. As one of the greatest, if not the greatest, ascended master, Jesus' story is available planet-wide for all to consider.

The message is clear. In order to access the genuinely miraculous, forgiveness is a requisite factor.

Perhaps you can forgive organized religion for distorting the story of Jesus Christ?

◎◎

NICK: Jesus is one of my favorite superheroes. Much is being said these days about whether or not Jesus even lived. As far as I'm concerned it doesn't even matter. What does matter is the teachings in the story. I can tell you this. I have carried a big man on my back whilst walking barefoot and unharmed over broken glass bottles. I have felt the *Grace* in scorching heat more than once firewalking naked upon red-hot coals. I have bent steel bars with my throat and challenged myself in many different ways. All of these milestones, these small and subtly powerful achievements, have initiated me into a deeper understanding of our *soul power*. In order to achieve these feats my highest form of meditation begins with the spiritual contemplation of the man Jesus nailed to the bloody wood—with so much compassion in his eyes. For me, this is a great benchmark to begin any form of inner journeying. Contemplation upon Jesus' story helps me access resources inside myself that are dynamic, receptive, intelligent, and very alive. Forgiveness, compassion—these core attitudes are the keys to the doorway which allows me to swiftly exit the normal waking state and experience the pure joy of *incension* (the ascension into the sacred heart within). The most relevant message Jesus came to share, for me, begins in that almighty act of compassion.

HO'O PONOPONO

A more recent example of the power of forgiveness is illustrated by the following true story as related by author of *The Attractor Factor* and cast member of the film *The Secret*, Joe Vitale.

Within this tale lies the inspiration that shatters a sense of individual powerlessness. Meditate deeply upon its meaning and apply the distillation of this contemplation to your way of being, for truly this tale reveals the magic potion to catalyze genuine invincibility.

Vitale describes:

Two years ago, I heard about a therapist in Hawaii who cured a complete ward of criminally insane patients—without ever seeing any of them. The psychologist would study an inmate's chart and then look within himself to see how he created that person's illness. As he improved himself, the patient improved.

When I first heard this story, I thought it was an urban legend. How could anyone heal anyone else by healing himself? How could even the best self-improvement master cure the criminally insane? It didn't make any sense. It wasn't logical, so I dismissed the story.

However, I heard it again a year later. I heard that the therapist had used a Hawaiian healing process called *Ho'o Ponopono*. I had never heard of it, yet I couldn't let it leave my mind. If the story was at all true, I had to know more. I had always understood "total responsibility" to mean that I am responsible for what I think and do. Beyond that, it's out of my hands.

I think that most people think of total responsibility that way. We're responsible for what we do, not what anyone else does—but that's wrong.

The Hawaiian therapist who healed those mentally ill people would teach me an advanced new perspective about total responsibility. His name is Dr. Ihaleakala Hew Len. We probably spent an hour talking on our first phone call. I asked him to tell me the complete story of his work as a therapist.

He explained that he worked at Hawaii State Hospital for four years. That ward where they kept the criminally insane was dangerous. Psychologists quit on a monthly basis. The staff called in sick a lot or simply quit. People would walk through that ward with their backs against the wall, afraid of being attacked by patients. It was not a pleasant place to live, work, or visit.

Dr. Len told me that he never saw patients. He agreed to have an office and to review their files. While he looked at those files, he would work on himself. As he worked on himself, patients began to heal.

"After a few months, patients that had to be shackled were being allowed to walk freely," he told me. "Others who had to be heavily medicated were getting off their medications. And those who had no chance of ever being released were being freed." I was in awe. "Not only that," he went on, "but the staff began to enjoy coming to work. Absenteeism and turnover disappeared. We ended up with more staff than we needed because patients were being released and all the staff was showing up to work. Today, that ward is closed."

This is where I had to ask the million-dollar question: "What were you doing within yourself that caused those people to change?"

"I was simply healing the part of me that created them," he said. I didn't understand. Dr. Len explained that total responsibility for your life means that everything in your life—simply because it is in your life—is your responsibility. In a literal sense the entire world is your creation.

Whew. This is tough to swallow. Being responsible for what I say or do is one thing. Being responsible for what everyone in my life says or does is quite another. Yet, the truth is this: if you take complete responsibility for your life, then everything you see, hear, taste, touch, or in any way experience is your responsibility because it is in your life. This means that terrorist activity, the president, the economy, or anything you experience and don't like—is up for you to heal. They don't exist, in a manner of speaking, except as projections from inside you. The problem isn't with them, it's with you, and to change them, you have to change you.

I know this is tough to grasp, let alone accept or actually live. Blame is far easier than total responsibility, but as I spoke with Dr. Len, I began to realize that healing for him and in *Ho'o Ponopono* means loving yourself.

If you want to improve your life, you have to heal your life. If you want to cure anyone, even a mentally ill criminal, you do it by healing you.

I asked Dr. Len how he went about healing himself. What was he doing, exactly, when he looked at those patients' files?

"I just kept saying, 'I'm sorry' and 'I love you' over and over again," he explained.

"That's it?"

"That's it."

◎◎

Let us reconsider the story of Captain John Newton. Newton was a slave trader. He sailed a ship to Africa and in some way participated in capturing the men of that land and women too, no doubt. And took them in chains for commercial gain across the sea and sold them. Many died en route—others were maimed.

The indigenous African people, some of them kings, some of them mothers and farmers, were taken from their land and dragged below deck on a ship bound for a hellish journey. They were taken to a foreign land in an act of cruel relocation and they were sold as property.

In order to achieve his historical destiny, Captain John Newton had to forgive himself completely for his crimes.

Yet the point is not only about who Newton was and what he did. This point is specifically about who we are. Consider how you are personally responsible for the crimes perpetrated on the planet. Ask yourself: "How am I responsible for these crimes?" Yes, you! That is *Ho'o Ponopono*. Ask yourself: "How am I responsible for oppressing the indigenous heart within me?" A natural part of ourselves has been plundered and ravaged by brutality for nothing more than loot—a short-term gain. We have fallen into a world of barbarism and need to forgive ourselves for this tragic turn of events.

As forgiveness is applied with the sincerity demonstrated by Dr. Hew Len in his *Ho'o Ponopono* practice, a new coding sequence is established within us. This code is akin to a combination lock, a *PIN* number, or secret password. It is an access code to above-top-secret clearance levels of natural security. With this code the door opens to the establishment of heaven upon Earth.

◎◎

NICK: For myself forgiveness has been a mountainous journey. I was taught a very different doctrine when I was a young lad, in the lonely fields of Lincolnshire, England. The men would very often bear a grudge. Forgiveness was not something that was easily and obviously practiced. Perhaps this poem I wrote best sums up my opinion of forgiveness:

THE RIVER OF LOVE

'Twas in the lonely years of flat Lincolnshire fields,
Where as a boy I ran wild and free,
That I dreamed the dreams of the man I wished so much to be.

The wind blew cold
And men grew old and talked of things that only their eyes could see.
Frosty mornings would bite,
Rain poured day and night, but no other place did I wish to be.

The fields, my home,
A river my teacher
And my best friends were trees and dogs.
My favourite music was the morning birds and the sound of
    burning logs.

I felt so alive, full of joy,
Happy just to be;
Not even the bullies with kick and punch could knock that joy
    from me;
But the most important thing a young lad needs,
In his home to keep him growing . . .
The River of Love,
Where this young fish swam, was slowly, slowly, slowing . . .

Fires of anger burned in the eyes of the man who called me his son;
My mother was sad, their love was cold, and froze in the years to
    come.
His temper was short,
His words were cruel and cut my heart with the ease of a knife;
My pain and fear then turned to spite
And 'twas my brother with whom I did fight.

All were deafened by the words of things that never were said,
They spoiled a love that hardly lived,
The family life was dead.

I was in a world I loved so much
But with which I would not deal and confused by things I did not
    know,
Yet inside of me could feel.

The tears I struggled to keep inside watered the wish in me,
To find my Self,
To be the man,
Someday I knew I could be;
So I said goodbye to those I loved
But never really knew
And wandered far from the fields where a lonely boy once grew.

Many a year I carried the pain
And dreamed of feeling peace again, and as I grew I understood,
We only did the best we could;
We can only teach what we've been shown and lessons of Love we'd
     hardly known.

Now today I see through clearer eyes,
This dream world of fears, ignorance, and lies.
And I hope one day all will see a simple Truth plain to me:
Now is the time to teach old and young
Lessons of Love,
So The River can run.

☺/☺

BREATHING FORGIVENESS

We need forgiveness—it is probably the only thing we need. That's the most important part in the jigsaw puzzle now. Some of us need a lot of forgiveness, applied liberally in every moment of every day. Forgiveness ... apply it. *Ho'o ponopono.* Heal the ward for the criminally insane.

How do you apply forgiveness all the time? By watering and nurturing the Ormus flower, by placing your attention on "the holy breath." If you truly wish to become a superhero and save the world from the hands of its molesters then get on with the joyful business of committing to maintaining the sweetest science. All you have to do is direct your consciousness towards the solution—all of the time.

Breathe forgiveness. When you drift off into other concerns, compassionately bring the focus back to the breath and breathe forgiveness into whatever floats across your consciousness.

Remember, joy is serious business in heaven. In the greatest story ever told, the victory of the underdog is what is required. It's a long shot. And victory is not guaranteed, that's the beauty of it.

THE NUDE WHIRLED WATER

According to some of the most enlightened Christian communicators, every time we judge we are driving the nails into the wrists of Jesus on the cross.

It is in the greatest challenges of our lives where forgiveness is applied that we rise out of the mire of judgment into another realm of response.

Our experience seems to support the idea that the difference between forgiveness (in all the ways mentioned) and judgment (e.g. negatively judging someone) is the difference between heaven and hell. The New World Order was a world based primarily on judgment. The Nude Whirled Water is a world based on forgiveness.

The conscious choice—to choose to enter into the mystery, to surrender all our judgments about ourselves, surrender all those and forgive, holy wholly, completely now and forever, the wrongs we have done to ourselves—must be applied at the deepest point of our inner feelings and thoughts. It is here, in this timeless realm, that one relinquishes understanding. This movement within one's own psyche is a gesture of integrity towards all humanity. As one creates peace within oneself, world peace is achieved. As inner disturbances disappear, the depth of the mystery becomes available for real omni-jective review. A true science is then born where evidence determines the theories instead of the present-day situation where theories determine the evidence.

THE JEDI DIRECTIVE

The activation of superhero capacity is our mission and Jedi directive. New Psalms are being sung and it is we who are singing them. The echoes of those hymns as they careen into the deep silence are being heard in the cosmos. Immortal yogis are taking their yoga into the stars. Through an attitude of righteousness the warrior is forged anew in the mythology of Valhalla.

Let's have fun for a moment.... Imagine (with your heart) launching into the celestial realms to ride alongside our cosmic brethren as a galactic explorer. Has your imagination brought you to consider a future role as a galactic citizen? What's happening out there in the cosmos anyway? Who is the president of the galaxy? Visualize us actually saving the planet at the last possible second. There must be an extraordinary celestial office up there for somebody who plays the critical role in what would have to be the greatest galactic caper of all time.

As we have mentioned, our friend Riley Martin, whom we consider to be a Martin Luther Cosmic King, has been up and down to the Biaviian Mothership on several occasions. Under Tan's directive he is drawing up and selling wayfarer soul tickets (symbols) into outer space like Uncle Remus on magic mushrooms. Check out www.riley-martin.tv and get your Jedi passport to the cosmos.

It is fascinating to consider that the Biaviians have destroyed two of their own worlds. What level of forgiveness did it take for these beings to get out of conflict? How many Jesuses died on their crosses?

@/@

Forgiveness—don't leave home without it!

@/@

DAVID: How do we get through life without judging? I do my best to abandon judgment and to use discernment instead. To me discernment means a decision without an emotional charge on it.

To illustrate this, I recall the story of a friend in my youth whom I considered to be a "bad drunk." He would cause all kinds of problems. When Friday or Saturday night came around, nobody wanted to be around him. He was literally a loose cannon every time alcohol touched his lips. And I often had to babysit his drunken escapades.

I loved the guy, he was a great friend, but he was a bad drunk. Others literally hated him because of his inability to control himself. Once I learned discernment, I was able to make decisions to avoid the guy on the weekends without getting caught in an emotionally charged exchange—without hate. To me that is discernment versus judgment.

@/@

The key attitudes and behaviors have been demonstrated by all the great teachers of antiquity and the superheroes and champions of the modern era. Forgiveness, compassion, the highest forms of love, gratitude, and innocent perception—all blended with the appropriate degrees of wonder and awe—allow us to exist in a simple state of being that exudes creativity and brings about the purest levels of personal health and happiness.

Forgiveness is a shamanic tool. As a consciously applied principle in life, forgiveness automatically and naturally triggers an opening to the mystery.

As we learn to utilize the energy of forgiveness, we become the powerful agents of change that we are being called to become—the superheroes of our time.

Let us hold true to the eternal superhero motto: Forgive and forget.

Forgiveness is a choice. It is a direction of consciousness. Forgiveness in our heart is always a choice in every situation.

"Consciousness seems proportionate to the living being's power of choice. It lights up the zone of potentialities that surrounds the act."

—Henri Bergson

"You must forgive those who hurt you, even if whatever they did to you is unforgivable in your mind. You will forgive them not because they deserve to be forgiven, but because you don't want to suffer and hurt yourself every time you remember what they did to you. It doesn't matter what others did to you. You are going to forgive them because you don't want to feel sick all the time. Forgiveness is for your own mental healing. You will forgive because you feel compassion for yourself. Forgiveness is an act of self-love."
—Don Miguel Ruiz, *The Mastery of Love*

Prayer of Personal Forgiveness

I bless this day and give thanks for my life.

Lord in Heaven, I am your child, your humble child.

I give you my love and thank you for your constant love and blessings.

Lord, I ask that you help me forgive and release, completely and totally, all people who have hurt me through thought, word or deed, knowing or not knowing.

Please Lord, please lord, thank you lord, thank you lord, thank you.

Lord in heaven, I ask that you help all people I have hurt through thought, word or deed, knowing or not knowing, to forgive and release me completely and totally.

Please Lord, please lord, thank you lord, thank you lord, thank you.

Lord, I ask that you help me forgive and release myself completely and totally, for all the times I hurt myself or hurt others through thought, word or deed, knowing or not knowing.

Please Lord, please Lord, thank you Lord, thank you Lord, thank you.

Lord in heaven, I ask that you help all life forms I have hurt, in any way at any time, to forgive and release me completely and totally.

Please Lord, please Lord, thank you Lord, thank you Lord, thank you.

Lord in heaven, I ask that you help me to be forgiven and released, completely and totally, for all my hurts or wrongs to the Earth and the life of the Earth through thought, word or deed, knowing or not knowing.

Please Lord, please Lord, thank you Lord, thank you Lord, thank you.

With this release, freedom, peace, power, and new life, I bless all creation in the entire universe and fill the entire universe with my love.

I love and bless the Earth, all life and all humanity; I love, bless, and respect the visible and the invisible.

I rejoice and give thanks for my new life, power, and health, and give complete blessings and love to all life, always.

Thank you Lord in Heaven, thank you Lord, thank you.

*This prayer was received from The Light by our friend Howard Wills.[10]

SUPERHERO ACTIVATION

"Anamnesis: All knowledge is remembering
what you always and forever know."
—PLATO

"Henceforth I ask not good-fortune; I myself am good-fortune."
—WALT WHITMAN

The time is ripe to access the true power of the soul and become *a superhero in the great drama of the ages.*

In Hopi Native American tradition, there is an ancient prophecy referring to the emergence of a tribe called *The Rainbow Warriors*. The prophecy foretold the destruction of their race and of the Earth and many of the birds and animals, etc. It also predicts the emergence of a group of individuals who, when the world is on the brink of absolute catastrophe, rise from the delusion of ignorance and become an embodiment of truth. The keynote of this prophecy was also the central theme of the messages of Jesus, Buddha, and many others who have borne witness to the extraordinary potential that lies within us all.

This tribe has no leader or political organization and is made up of people from all nations, religions, and cultures. The members of this tribe are united in spirit, in consciousness; their mission is to transform themselves by being a living embodiment of their calling and by holding a golden vision—the vision of paradise on Earth.

Everywhere throughout the world are scattered the seeds of this tribe. If you truly desire to make a difference and, in this exciting time of extraordinary opportunity, lend the full weight of your soul purpose to creating paradise on Earth, then simply decide to become a Rainbow Warrior—otherwise known as a superhero.

The great call of this age is to activate the archetype of the superhero—an archetype that was placed within our hearts by the forces of natural goodness through cartoons, comic books, films, novels, and art. All that is required is to have the courage to recover, with God's grace, your true, natural self.

❀❀

In the epic tale played out in the life, crucifixion, and resurrection of Jesus Christ, the superhero archetype was established in the collective human consciousness. Jesus' whole life was a demonstration of what *we all may achieve.* It was the demonstration of fully incarnate human potential. It is time to strip away the nonsense that politically organized religion and fiendish powers have attempted to wire into our souls. Christ-consciousness itself, speaking through the mouth of Jesus, said that those who follow His way would accomplish even greater things than He.

"Verily, verily, I say unto you, He that believeth on me, the works that I do shall he do also; and greater works than these shall he do; because I go unto my Father."
—JESUS CHRIST, JOHN 14:12

"Is it not written in your law, I said, Ye are gods?"
—JESUS CHRIST, JOHN 10:34

❀❀

THE SECRET POWER OF PAIN

All that is written on these pages may be so many words, and one may be driven to ask, "What about the pain?" "What about the suffering?" "What about our sins?" "How does a being in pain become a superhero?"

To this we restate the Zen proverb: "Pain is inevitable. Suffering is optional." And we revisit the astonishing insight of Nietzsche when he wrote: "It is by being wounded that power grows and in the end can become tremendous." Let us not be naïve. Without rain, there are no rainbows. At every success level, we are met by a different devil.

There is that great Doors song, where Jim Morrison sings: "I've been down so God damn long that it looks like up to me."[11] And of course there is the death-defying story of the Africans chained below deck on Captain John Newton's ship. We have all been so far down in the hole at various stages of our life, lives, past lives, collective realities, etc., that we have arrived at a choice. We can consciously choose to no longer feel the emotions of loss, guilt, sadness, or depression. These emotions do nothing but destroy. Plus, there are enough people on the planet feeling terrible. *God is looking for volunteers who want to feel great always.* It is up to us to balance out all the negative emotions on the planet by consciously choosing to feel only positive emotions all the time.

◎◎

"Every master was once a disaster."
—Anonymous

◎◎

If we meditate on our pain and ask our Creator for help, we eventually become aware of three hidden aspects of our pain—each following the other.

First, we become aware of what is wrong. Understanding this seems obvious, yet we are continuously astounded that persistent stomachaches do not cause people to change their diets.

Second, we become aware of actions we can take to fix it. This can be an intense process, especially if we are wound up deeply in an illusion (lies we have bought into), emotional excesses (anger, hate, etc.), unresolved burdens (negative karma), and other parasites on our soul. The unwinding process may take some deep soul-searching.

Third, we become aware that our pain can be a tremendous transformative catalyst of our own consciousness. The trials of pain and suffering can turn an individual from a moron into a genius. Genius consists of developing certain aspects of consciousness that include the following:

1. Knowing one's mission and daily taking action in alignment with that mission.
2. Focusing only on thoughts that strengthen.
3. The ability to relate and communicate with others in a heartwarming, loving way.
4. The ability to demonstrate competency by efficiency.
5. Knowing where to get knowledge when it is required.
6. Knowing how to organize relevant knowledge into definite plans of action.
7. Acting always from a place of joy, love, and laughter.

We believe that, of those listed, the most important aspect of genius—the aspect that makes all the other elements of genius achievable—is completely aligning one's soul with one's mission in life.

☺☺

"Yes. I believe sincerely that every man has consummate genius within him. Some appear to have it more than others only because they are aware of it more than others are, and the awareness or unawareness of it is what makes each one of them into masters or holds them down to mediocrity. I believe that mediocrity is self-inflicted and genius is self-bestowed. Every successful man I have ever known, and I have known a great many, carries with him the key which unlocks that awareness and lets in the universal power that has made him into a master."

—WALTER RUSSELL

DHARMA: YOUR MISSION

"Follow your bliss. . . . Any life career that you choose in following your bliss should be chosen with that sense—that nobody can frighten me off from this thing. And no matter what happens, this is the validation of my life and action."

—JOSEPH CAMPBELL WITH BILL MOYERS, *THE POWER OF MYTH*

Everyone performs with absolute brilliance in some area of their daily lives. Everyone has a super power of some sort that when developed becomes the symbol of their superhero status. This power is the ability that allows one's mission to be accomplished. It is a special skill.

What is your special skill?

What is it that you do better than anyone else?

In what field do you excel?

As you answer these questions we recommend that you pour everything you've got into these strengths. We are designed to perfect our strengths, not tinker with our weaknesses. In perfecting our strengths, we automatically overcome our weaknesses.

What specific career inspires and captivates your heart?

What kind of work causes all time to disappear for you?

What career would you do even if you were not paid?

As you answer these questions we recommend that you utilize your strengths while moving towards your ideal career. Your ideal career is your mission.

Remember: where our heart lies, there too will our treasures be found.

ᐤᐤ

For some their life's mission may be as simple as a core soul realization of perfection in the universe and the sharing of that truth. For others it may be the physical and psychic transformation into a superhero, with all the adventure that entails. For others it may be a metamorphosis into an earth-spirit-love soldier whose end goal is paradise on Earth. For others it might mean total peace as the best parent ever. For some the mission is to become the most eco-friendly business person on the planet—an example for all to emulate.

Fully embrace your purpose, your mission, your dharma. You can be a full-on, front-line undercover agent for global transformation that keeps life exciting on this spinning planet. This requires being your authentic self. Being 100% who you really are is a vastly entertaining career—without a doubt, the best career ever.

Consider that we are not simply activating our mission within a modern material world; we are activating our mission within the context of a material world in an extraordinary and, perhaps, unprecedented period of total and complete transformation. Our former station as spiritual tourists here on Earth now shifts into the fulfillment of our cosmic destiny. By channeling our power into action (based on our individual unique mission) and being directed by our sacred heart with an attitude of forgiveness, we step into our role as an official planetary superhero.

As a superhero, there is no telling what the Light has in store for you. Yet we may guess that our ultimate destiny is beyond anyone's wildest imagination.

ᐤᐤ

"When you are inspired by some great purpose, some extraordinary project, all your thoughts break their bounds. Dormant forces,

faculties and talents become alive, and you discover yourself to be a greater person by far than you ever dreamed yourself to be."
—PATANJALI

As a superhero, one is recognized by his or her outfit. Of course every superhero must be known to the public by their outfit—their fashion statement. Yet be careful to avoid being distracted from the truth: of all the things you wear, your expression is the most important.

People like to associate with people who are fun, so a smile and a pleasing personality are mandatory for any superhero.

◎◎

INNOCENT PERCEPTION

Innocent perception is a perspective that strengthens one's power as a superhero. Become your own expert.

The Hawaiian phrase *"A'ohe pau ka 'ike i ka halau ho'okahi"* means "All knowledge is not taught in one school." This is a variation on the idea that there are many sources of knowledge and always many different viewpoints.

In the pursuit of any goal, innocent perception teaches us that all ways of knowing should be considered: direct experience, meditative, intuitive, psychic, kinesthetic, channeled, dreaming, as well as empirical trials and experimental methods. The primary viewpoint amongst many is direct experience. All knowledge of reality begins with one's direct experience.

Be alert. Review your experience with a lens of innocent perception. What is your direct experience really telling you about:

> the Galaxy?
> the Solar System?
> the Sun?
> the Moon?
> the rain?

the oceans?

the human experience?

the qualities of love?

your goals?

the qualities of plants?

the nature of dirt and soil?

the nature of water?

the nature of fire?

the nature of air?

the power of forgiveness?

These are important points to appreciate and are worth recording in your journal with at least two- or three-sentence responses to each question.

THE TECHNOLOGY OF SUPER-HUMAN POTENTIAL

DAVID: The collapsing worlds of centralized television programming, junk food, box living, materialism, and absurd legislation have left unprecedented opportunities in their wake. We live today in a world of unlimited resources and unlimited wealth—exactly the opposite of what we've been told. We live in a world where alchemistry is real— where lead can be turned into the white powder of gold! The fact that individuals every day create incredible value out of almost nothing— go from rags to riches almost overnight—is proof positive that radical transformation is possible for anyone at any time. The device that allows instantaneous and radical change is technology. I'm not talking just about cars, trucks, computers, televisions, and cellular phones— I'm talking about another type of technology, the technology of human potential. This technology includes audio-tape learning, download-able self-empowering MP3 files from the Internet, the mass distribution of self-improvement and nutrition books, success videotapes, relationship-transforming information, spiritual media of all types, wealth-development literature, etc. All of these are simple tools that can radically enhance the quality of your life instantly. We all have an infinite number of choices of what we can focus on. *The superhero deliberately selects to focus on the technology of super-human potential as much as superhumanly possible.* The technology of super-human potential creates the maximum possibility of return on the investment of your time.

Nick and I trust that the ideas in this book have brought into view exactly how great each individual's potential really is by taking an in-depth look at our status and location in the cosmos as best as we can understand it. Our goal is that you discover with us that at the leading edge of awareness is an exciting, inspirational, radical, enjoyable, and practical platform of all possibilities.

Superhero Consciousness

The superhero is not a politician who attempts to convince anyone of anything. The very existence of the superhero is the message.

Consider that in nearly every case each "truth" since the beginning of history (that we were convinced was the gospel) has been proven, over time, to be inaccurate, flawed, incomplete, or simply ridiculous. Yet each generation clings to these truths as if they were clutching for their very lives. Eventually the wave of new information sweeps away the old paradigm, and the next generation clings to the new paradigm with all its might.

"A new scientific truth does not triumph by convincing its opponents and making them see the light, but rather because its opponents eventually die, and a new generation grows up that is familiar with it."
—Max Planck, mathematician, physicist

"The free, expansive vision is molded into the institutional. Hardly has the institutional mortar set before there is a new cortical upheaval, an explosive, often ecstatic or prophetic revelation. The prophet is promptly jailed. A hundred years later his followers are jailing the next visionary."

—TIMOTHY LEARY, *THE POLITICS OF ECSTASY*

❀❀

The superhero does not ask what to believe but instead wonders: "What is it useful to believe?"

What can you believe that would allow you to feel incredible all the time?

What beliefs can you adopt now that would cause you to laugh the most?

❀❀

A young man spent many years in search of enlightenment, but it eluded him. Then one day as he strolled through the market square, he overheard a conversation between a fruit seller and a customer. "Give me the best piece of fruit you have," said the customer. And the fruit seller replied, "Every piece of fruit I have is the best fruit ever. There is no piece of fruit here that is not the best ever." Upon hearing this, the young man became enlightened.

❀❀

THE PATH OF MASTERY: COMMUNICATION SKILLS

Activating our superpowers, fully enjoying the depths of living, and developing the type of transformative relationships hinted at by *ALOHA* require excellent communication skills.

Of all skills, the superhero must master communication. The number-one wealth habit, the greatest commodity of the ultra-prosperous, is having excellent communication skills. At all levels of achievement, the great communicators will be found at the top. Is it a coincidence that public speaking is one of the highest-paid professions?

Great communicators learned in their youth the power and beauty of the voice. They say "Please" and "Thank you." They are courteous and treat people with respect. They treat each individual in front of them as if they were the most important person in the world. Great communicators use non-violent communication and seek a win-win strategy in negotiations. Swearing is avoided. The *ALOHA* spirit is felt in the tone of their voice. They forgive swiftly and communicate that forgiveness clearly.

Skilled communicators take full responsibility for both sides of the communication. They never assume that someone understands. They always double-check. They are acutely aware of how others are reacting to their words.

The best communicators understand that the very best thing you can give someone is what they want. However, discovering what someone wants requires clever communication!

Let it be clear: The spoken word has always been the motivating factor that establishes the great cathedrals, the sacred temples, the grand movements of human potential, the bountiful levels of prosperity felt by millions throughout the world, the freedoms we enjoy, the joyous spiritual revolutions.

NEVER TELL ME THE ODDS

Even with air pollution, water pollution, soil pollution, food poison, etc., at all-time highs, modern science (as a front for greedy energy-control corporations financed by Illuminati banking interests) still has nearly everyone fooled.

Can we save the planet? Can we actually achieve peace on Earth? Can we clean the planet up of all the toxic waste? Can we clean all the toxic waste out of ourselves? Practically everybody says it is impossible based on their indoctrination by modern science. Worse still, it appears, that nearly everyone *believes* deep down in the impossibility. Day by day the peril to our planet continues to mount.

Do you recall Han Solo's immortal words in the *Star Wars* film *The Empire Strikes Back* after C3PO tells him the impossibility of successfully navigating an asteroid field? "Never tell me the odds" is what he said.

No matter how impossible it may appear, the superhero requires not one other person's belief that we can turn the situation around; only their own faith and certainty are needed. The superhero knows the power of the X-factor and that spontaneous healing is always possible. The superhero knows that the solutions to today's problems have already been found. The superhero protects, nurtures, and helps deliver the imminent free-energy technologies into mass consciousness and mass availability, knowing that the very existence of such technologies reveals a basic truth and in one fell swoop collapses the ivory towers of lies.

In essence, the superhero continues to move forward completely undaunted in what may one day be remembered as the greatest love story ever told, namely: how we turned the biggest disaster ever into paradise on this Earth in a galactic cliff-hanger of unparalleled proportions—a turnaround so baffling that even the aliens were left completely stunned as to the true depth, beauty, majesty, manifestation power, love, and patience found within the human soul.

☉/☉

THE POWER OF PATIENCE (TRUST, STILLNESS, FAITH)

NICK: If we want to become a superhero and, in so doing, triumph over distortion and disharmony within us ... If we choose to rise in our mythology and summon the power of our ancestors' dreams and hopes and harness all that they fought and died for, and sculpt ourselves in the flow of destiny as an immortal hero in the battle against the forces of evil ... If we dare to come down from those hills of innocence and slay Goliath ... then ... we will, as King David's story illustrates, be required to embody certain qualities. These dynamic qualities are the virtues of the saints and the building blocks of the superhero character. We feel those qualities are best shared in stories.

Apart from courage, conviction, intuition, relationship with Spirit, innocence, and other virtues of the superhero, one of the least under-stood qualities and perhaps least emphasized is patience. As much as forgiveness is a core element of compassion, patience is a core element of innocence. Patience with its delicate accoutrements of trust, stillness, and faith is required in order to recreate optimal harmonics within our reality. Sooner or later we are going to be tested for patience. Con-sider the following tale:

> I remember a while back in Spanish Africa I was living high in the ravine of an ancient mystical mountain. On the ocean side of the mountain pass were timeless cliffs of sheer basalt rocks rising like the inside of some gigantic volcano. Some gypsies from South America lived below me and had tapped into the aquifer beneath the bedrock. Once a week I would descend from my camp to fetch water from their constantly running pipe.
>
> The well-watered land was a mini oasis in a barren and sharp rocky landscape. The gypsies had large bamboo clumps, maybe thirty feet in girth, and around one of these clumps was chained a most foreboding and vicious beast. The name of the creature was Bull, and a more aptly named animal one would be hard-pressed to find. Bull was a fighting dog, bred for the pit by old-school cut-throats, thick-armed shady fellows with whom I had nothing to do, who sat in their doorways on burning hot after-noons with sad-looking women dressed all in black. A cross between a Great Dane and the Pit Bull terrier, a *Lanzarote Prezzer* is a fearsome beast indeed. All dark, nasty and primal with a gigantic square head not unlike the countenance of the puff adder (one of the most deadly and intimidating snakes in the world), Bull was equipped to maim with extreme ferocity.
>
> One day as I was fetching water, Bull broke his leather col-lar, which had become dry and brittle in the baking African sun. With his owners away Bull stalked me, an intruder upon his turf.

Now, every word of what follows is true. This was an initiation through fear for the teller of this tale.

I was sitting in a half squat enjoying the warm breeze on my body. Bare-skinned, barefooted, I was taking my time filling the bottles I had. I suddenly felt uneasy, as if some extraordinary presence was approaching from behind. A cold, slow-moving wave was pushing into the field of awareness to my rear, and I turned slowly to see what it was. I found myself looking into the soul of Bull. If you can imagine the gates of Hades and the 3-headed dog Cerberus guarding the mouth of hell, then this is a good starting place to join me as Bull moved very, very slowly closer towards me, drooling, growling in a soft, rumbling, primal tone, every muscle of his 150-pound frame cocked and loaded, ready to spring terrible bear-like into a fight. The only thing I heard in my mind was "Don't move." Moments passed, which became minutes. The water overflowed the bottle. I was in half squat, thighs beginning to burn, my thin sarong flapping softly in the breeze, its flimsy movement a stark contrast to the terror the moment contained.

Fear can conjure up a dreadful monster of thought, a true Goliath, and if ever the substance was present from which to form some dreadful possibility, my mind had all the clay it could need. But thoughts are controllable and in that moment I didn't have the luxury of using them improperly. I recalled the tale of Odysseus who, when attacked by dogs, sat down on the ground to show them he was no threat. His surrender disengaged their attack. I thought about this. Yet for me, at that instant, the voice had been very clear. Do not move.

Bull moved closer, inches navigated with primordial predatory ferocity, his fights in the pit filling his biology with cellular readiness, teeth dripping yellow, twitching on the blocks, waiting for the gun, which was any movement from me—the signal to unleash his savage, dark, primordial fury. Have you ever seen a dog like this? Can you imagine a creature with an instinct to clamp on with the jaws and not let go until death?

Great Danes are the biggest dogs and pit bulls are among the most vicious and tenacious. The challenge to remain still went on to the point of my legs beginning to tremble in their half squat. I decided to adjust as slowly as possible. As soon as the first micro movement was detected by my terrifying friend, he struck into me with full ferocity like some silver back gorilla marking his turf. He took three quick vicious snaps through my sarong, aiming for my testicles and penis. The first snap opened up three-quarters of an inch wound on the outer skin of my penis, and blood immediately spurted out. "Don't move!" was still the objective as I did a quick hip jerk of which Chubby Checker would have been proud, saving my privates from a grisly fate, and probably my bleeding to death by their loss. Still not having moved my feet, twisting into a more upright position, 'twas at this point I moved my right hand a little. Bull immediately snapped again at the movement and my middle fingernail was somehow ripped completely off. This was an extraordinary situation. Blood gushing from my wound, fire finger burning, there we were, now his big square head pressed against the back of my left thigh, canine fangs against my flesh, growling all death and ferocity.

His head was resting against an old wound, an injury from childhood days when fear had made me cling to a rope we were swinging around on, and instead of dropping into the corn below I held on and bashed into the iron girder on the side of the shed and was knocked twenty feet, landing hard on the edge of a sharp cold brick wall. It was a pain so terrible I can scarcely describe. My leg has been deformed with a hole in the hamstring ever since.

Today, however, fear was not to be the victor. The patience and conviction required "not to move" paid off. Like a matador in his dainty silk slippers, there I stood waiting, refusing to move any more. Eventually, thank God, Bull, sensing the wrongness of what he had done, disengaged.

I stood trembling, bleeding badly, but in my mind a Goliath was dead at my feet. Not Bull, but something even more tenacious—impatience—was gone from my life.

"Infinite patience is the only thing that gets immediate results."
—A COURSE IN MIRACLES

In light of this tale we arrive at another hidden theme: Inevitably, we will stand before the beast. We will gaze the beast directly in the eye. This must happen if we are to fully experience the depths of life as the climactic chapters unfold of the greatest love story ever told. For our true power is birthed through tribulation. Ascension is preceded by descent. No rain, no rainbows. No night, no stars. We know the true depth of our courage as we confront our worst fears. We experience the true nature of our purity as we deal with the worst toxicity. This is the way of the world.

The superhero steps into the arena with the beast in the flow of Grace and virtue, armed and ready for battle. Consider just a few of the weapons of love that the superhero wields: patience, innocence, trust, stillness, faith, certainty, gratitude, peace, surrender, the best attitude ever, awareness, etc.

With this in mind, we see that the climax of the greatest story ever told starts to take on absurd and astonishing richness and feeling as a clash of the titans becomes inevitable.

WE DARE YOU!

Behold the Age of Confluence. Titanic forces are converging and an extraordinary vista is opening up before us all.

We now know that the reality we experience as our world is being sculpted by ALL of us. Literally, every single one of us is causing the experience we share on this planet Earth.

"For we wrestle not against flesh and blood, but against principal-
ities, against powers, against the rulers of the darkness of this
world, against spiritual wickedness in high places."
—EPHESIANS 6:12

We also know, however, that the thoughts, words, and actions as well
as subsequent feeling states of the Earth's entire population are being
infected and manipulated by seriously malevolent forces working
through the machinations of banking, chemical agriculture, mass
media, energy production industries, organized religion, and political systems. The whole direction of civilization has been and is being
specifically engineered by the most toxic beings in our world.

   This fact alone is fuelling a growing anger in the human collective as more and more individuals awaken to the shocking truths
behind all hidden government agendas and the appalling consequences, which we witness in the world as state-sponsored terrorism,
psycho-spiritual warfare, pollution, toxicity, synthetic drugs, war, etc.

   Mythologically and archetypally, anger is often referred to as *red
energy*. Part of the initiation for The Warrior Hero is to harness the
power of red energy and channel it for the most productive and effective outcome. Anger and rage suppressed will eventually surface in
some war somewhere outside the individual or manifest as a disease
within. Anger harnessed and transmuted into passion for the transformation of the ordinary into the extraordinary is one of the most
potent catalysts in the alchemical shape-shift, transmutation, trans-
figuration that the superhero may undergo.

   These are challenging times, because they must be. Just as a butterfly emerging from the cocoon has to endure a struggle in order to
free itself, so do we. Without that struggle the butterfly cannot develop
the strength in its wings to fly. It is up to each one of us to use anger
to escape our own cocoons and then to harness our emotional intensity to fly forward on our mission as we become the embodiment of the
living solution.

   In order to achieve this, superheroes know they must follow the path of their highest destiny, answer their true calling in life, and activate wholly their full potential in the world. Whatever the so-called "negative" emotion, the superhero will accept and harness its power to fuel her or his resolve and perseverance to align thoughts, words, and actions with her or his highest calling in Life.

@/@

"What we feel, we attract. What we imagine, we become."
—Dr. Maxwell Maltz

@/@

As the manifestations of evil become more and more clear and the shock factor registers, we are well advised to see the opposite possibility: beings of great goodness, love, and unselfish benevolence have the opportunity to appear in the world. The shocking and horrific revelations of demonic energies associated with many Illuminati conspiracy theories propel superheroes into a state of superconsciousness.

The superhero understands that, at present, within the great human drama, a battle is raging. It is a battle between the forces of Light and Darkness for the possession of infinitely creative Soul Power. It is only Soul Power that shapes and sculpts creation into form. Through thoughts, words, and actions and the consequential feeling states, realities are engineered and worlds are formed. The timing into and beyond 2012 is of immense significance. Life is rearranging the props on the stage and a new scene is beginning. Our challenge is to activate our mission, protect the last sovereign territory of the original world (our soul-heart-mind), and then enjoy the ride. As the new world order fries, the old world order revives—wiser.

The souls of angels and gods, heroes and superheroes are stirring. A moment approaches that will be heard ringing down through the ages. Join forces with every superhero alive in the final act of the greatest love story ever told. Our allies include everything natural: Gaia, all plants and superplants, all animals, the wind, living waters, rocks, stones, gems, and crystals, invisible and visible supernatural beings, brothers and sisters from the stars, our own almighty feelings of love and compassion, and a strength and purity of soul-heart-mind sculpted in the waters of introspection.

In order to successfully navigate the troubled waters within, the superhero focuses the lens of introspection with great dexterity and skill. A confused population seeded with manifestations of evil is the landscape we survey, but our focal point is intensely concentrated on the good, the all-powerful, the unstoppable, the victorious—in essence, the mission that exists within us.

The superhero knows that movement to confront the inner-outer beast is futile without her/his *soul power*—Source. Without this the foe is far too mighty. Skywalker cannot face Vader without mastering The Force. Jesus cannot face the cross without his connection to The Father, and we cannot face ourselves without the Amazing Grace that surrounds and penetrates every fiber of our being.

The time is now to fully awaken to the mechanics of reality creation. Taking responsibility for the world we perceive around us is as wonderful as it is shocking, as fantastic as it is horrific. We can no longer hide behind the sanitized illusion of a material world that causes so much war, toxicity, and disease. The time is upon us (as Shakespeare so eloquently put it) to "take arms against the sea of troubles." The *Titanic* has hit the iceberg and is going down. Feng shui and rearranging the furniture are not enough. Another strategy is called for.

Controlling forces and the Legion of Doom are bombarding us daily with strategies designed to prevent our divine reunion—our own alchemical wedding. We know the normal waking state allows us to experience about 2% of our available capacity. This is a counterfeit experience of what it means to be alive. The Illuminati are designing a world populated by the living dead—zombie slaves divorced from their own Source.

Yet—a great awakening is upon us all. This awakening from the slumber of the hypnotic effect of messages crafted by false masters requires a sobering digestion of extraordinary information. Rolling over and trying to carry on sleeping is no longer an option. David has to face Goliath. Captain John Newton has to steer the ship through the storm. Jesus has to face the cross. Skywalker has to meet Vader. Arjuna has to fight his battle, and we have to face ourselves.

The stage is set for the greatest act ever in the cosmic play of the eons. In the hero's quest, success is not guaranteed. No one can say for sure what will happen. What is at stake is the entire planet. Even now battles are being fought on the fringes of our imagination for possession of our all-powerful ability to create. The stakes are the highest ever.

Nothing short of an X-Factor miracle is going to make this a story with a happy ending.

Fortunately, X-Factor miracles are the business of the superhero. The superhero calls upon cosmic forces within and beings from the heavens whom, even now, move amongst us and are here to help. The superhero knows that meditating inside the inspiration of one's soul power and dharma in all one's thoughts, words, and deeds can summon the allies, the shocking synchronicities, the harrowing escapes, the outrageous turns of fate, the twists in the plot, the shields of protection, the slight edge in the final confrontation that will deliver victory at the last possible second in the greatest love story ever told.

"He that dwelleth in the secret place of the most High shall abide under the canopy of protection of the Almighty."
—Psalm 91

Now armed with the guidebook to becoming a superhero, you can take your stand in the greatest love story ever told and consciously slay the Goliath within you with a merciless blow of compassion. If ever there was a time to activate your full human potential and rejoice in love-soaked gratitude, this is it.

We dare you to step forth onto centerstage.

This is your scene, your moment, your opportunity to shine forth the powers of your soul before your greatest fans. This is the time to take heroic, sacred action as the superhero you are and were always destined to be.

To go from long shot to legend is what God is asking you to do.

Today, go forth and win. The world loves an underdog. Along your journey, many will challenge you, object to you, struggle against you ... and yet, when you achieve your dreams there will be a roar of applause from the universe. And when you do, let that moment cast its magic upon your eternal soul forever.

We dare you to make today the best day ever.

Never was there a more illustrious time to be alive. This is the best life ever. This is the best year ever. This is the best day ever. This is the best moment ever. Superheroes live everyday as if it were their last and live everyday as if it were their first. The superhero knows in their soul that the best day ever is a state of vision, a feeling of consciousness, a momentous summary of being in the flow with all that is good in the world.

May the angels guide you as you take your rightful place in an astonishing tale of intrigue, romance, hope, and superheroism. May it be a sacred adventure. We herald your entry into the ranks of the planetary superheroes who are here to transform the Earth into the best planet ever.

May God bless us ALL.

๑๑

"We, the unwilling, led by the unknowing, are doing the impossible for the ungrateful. We have done so much, for so long, with so little, we are now qualified to do anything with nothing."
—MOTHER TERESA

"There is no difficulty that enough Love will not conquer; no disease that enough Love will not heal; no door that enough Love will not open; no gulf that enough Love will not bridge; no wall that enough Love will not throw down; no sin that enough Love will not redeem.... It makes no difference how deeply seated may be the troubles. How hopeless the outlook. How muddled the tangle; how great the mistake. A sufficient realization of Love will dissolve it all. If only you could Love enough you would be the happiest and most powerful being in the world."

—EMMET FOX

SELECTED POETRY

THE POEM OF TAN

RECITED TO RILEY MARTIN
BY O-QUA TANGIN WANN (A.K.A. TAN)

I have traveled far and swiftly, across yon deep and leaning sky:
I have witnessed a nova's burst, and saw a living planet die.
Across the voids of space unmeasured, Oh yea, Omsa-La-Juwann:
I have pierced the quantum octaves, mastered hyper-warps in time.

Vaulting onward o'er the spiral, on a journey here to save:
Fellow beings wrought of madness, from yon weeping, living grave.
Nestled there upon the ether, as a jewel among the stones:
Earth the precious orb of legend, soon your glowing shall be done.

Children of the living waters, possessors of the staff of reason:
Beings of celestial promise, doomed to perish in mid-season.
From the stone axe to the heavens, lo' the vision did not fade:
Still that pulsing seed of hatred, lay thy fate beneath the spade.

Before me the planet lay in shambles, eco-destruction beyond
    repair:
By the greed of false controllers, acids now permeate the air.
Pristine waters from the mountains, die en route down to the sea:
Thus to hasten soon the horror, the sapien race may cease to be.

All my dreams of bio-perfection, were but a futile deed:
Seeking to create a pure utopia, we unleashed a monster seed.
Still within them lay the spirit to transcend the rabid beast:
And to comprehend the Omsa of the elements of peace.

Oh ye marvels of creation, why have you not sought the light:
Must you fade into the shadows of that still, cold, azure night?
Unto you my sign is written, there upon the living fields.
Lo' the circle is eternal, though you perish, you yet shall live.

Interfacing with the acids, beneath some new Jurassic sea:
To turn again and scan the heavens, and to learn again to be, to be.
If I did not breach your stratus, you would surely some day breach
    mine:
'Tis a factor without question, 'tis a factor but of time.

I have not returned to conquer, nor to alter the flow of fate:
But simply to gather a certain number, before it is too late.
Too unstable to embrace, yet far too noble to cast away:
Beautiful life form though unsuccessful, might succeed another
    day:
There upon the flowering meadows, Oh, shining precious Biaveh.

THE SILENT RIVER

BY NICK GOOD

There is a Silent River in our lives
    we must surely follow
with courage and knowing
all is well
on and to tomorrow.

Carried we are, never alone
    by Its perfect Force and tide;
try we must
to have the strength
to let go and flow with the ride.

Born we are, One and All,
    into and from Its Nature
boundless and free
like The River are we
if we go to where It would take us.

Sisters and brothers
    we have but lost
all sight of the invisible Force
and sit on the banks of our dry souls
wishing for something to direct our course.

But all the while we live and breathe
    in the waters of eternal knowing.
The Silent River runs wild and free,
unknown ... It feeds our growing.

If we all live in this mad world
    unaware we are part of The Source,
what new world shall we create
when we open to Its beauty filled Force?

Sisters and brothers open mind and heart
    let The River flood without from within,
arid the valley old ones have left
young fish now have to live in.

And we, no better than their like,
    if we wait to be shown The Way,
now is the time to join the many
learning of Truth today.

The River is Life, the essence of all,
    never-ending and natural change
that is our Nature
baptized in the waters,
all become *The Saved*.

Acknowledge The Spirit,
    the Source of Life,
the only thing that will always exist;
no one can discover
The Force of Life
if Its current they try to resist.

Just sit in peace
    by the banks of Self,
listen to thy waters run;
calm the flow of your thoughts,
let a Silent River come.

Breathe and know,
    trust that you are
all a Great River should be;
alive and pure,
clean and strong,
wild and truly free.

THE PLANET EARTH

BY DAVID WOLFE

The stately planets
Spread like pearls.
In the cosmic space
These celestial worlds.

And we are here
On this spinning sphere:
The great Earth of cerulean oceans,
Always mixing, fixing
Enchanted potions.

Consider . . . . . .
All the splendor of this fantastic world:
The majesty of hollowed waves curled,
Deserts, savannah, scrublands,
Prairies, orchards, parklands,
Woods, dunes, and sands,
Montane forestlands,
Frigid polar zones,
Volcanic cones,
Tropical jungles, bare steppes,
Deep ocean trench depths.

Imagine . . . . . .
All the grace and strength
Across the Earth's length
Of billions of beasts, birds, fish, and trees;
The beauty of the island seas
Surrounded by fluke tails,
Luminescent whales.
White sand beaches of priceless worth
With wild white horses galloping across the surf.

Gaia,
You are this Earth.
You are the miracle of birth.
You are the mother of all.
You are this spinning ball
Poised out in space,
Protected by grace.

You reproduce with such splendor
Flowers, pollen, every gender.
Seed to shoot
To lengthening root
To stem to leaf
To fruit to seed.
You gift us all we need.

Your seeds bounce and roll,
Planting themselves with intention, soul.
Your seeds travel by wind, wing,
Causing all the birds to sing.
Your seeds, indeed
May be eaten with fruit,
Protected by a skin suit,
Moved out, fertilized,
Sprouted, realized.
Some seeds are carried, hidden,
And grow there—forgotten.
Your seeds float on the seas
Or sail gently on the breeze.

This planet
Is never static.
Always changing
The landscape rearranging.
Lakes and pools dry out,
Volcanoes throw stones about,
Continents may rip,
The Earth-crust can slip.

Always creating
More rarified forms
In laboratories of wind,
Rain, lightning storms.

Gaia, you have
Sculpted yourself into shining canyons.
Tangled yourself in the roots of banyans.
Ever repatterned yourself and grown.
Formed trees from solid stone.
Distilled drops through leaves, fruits, flowers
With so many hidden powers.
Contrived startling fragrances
In pollen, petals, and herbage.

Who could strip the Earth
Of her mystery?
Who could know the Earth's true history?

Submerged continents have disappeared
And lies are taught that we've endeared—feared;
Truths are always stranger than fiction
Buried by Gaia's skin-crust friction.

Yet megalith-memories still stand
On ancient holy lands.
Mystic sounds
On burial grounds
Where shamans danced,
And buffalo pranced,
Where all had come to be,
Where we could see,
Something we couldn't see,
With your plant chemicals,
And minerals.
Alkaloids, ephemeral
Entheogenic, seminal.

Consider ......
Ocean air, volcanic dust.
Pine floors filled with rust.
The flowery meadows and shady groves.
Vast silent forests, where Sasquatch roves.
Distant lands of fire and snow,
And midnight sun where hot springs flow.

The fleecy clouds,
And vapor shrouds,
The swaying rain,
The gentle dew.

Looking into a drizzling lake,
I see you.

Gaia,
Your temper explodes in volcanic fury.
Your laughter radiates in tropical sun.
Your tears pour in heavy rains.
Your bliss emanates in silent deserts.
Your roar bursts in thunderstorms.
Your confidence exudes from mountains.
Your anger soars in hurricanes.
Your grace calms in wild orchards.
Your confusion spins in tornadoes.
Your love embraces in gentle summer winds.

You perspire life.

Could ever there be too much wonder
In the simple spark of lightning, thunder?

A mountain is more
Than a mine of ore;
It is our strength, our core.
A river is more
Than water, sand;

It is the veins of the land.
A forest is more
Than a paper war;
It is our roof, walls, floor.

Observe
Gaia forgiving.
Think of the gifts Gaia's giving,
To live the life you are living.

Feel ......
That you are barefoot running
Naked, breathing.
Charging through forest, bending up turf.
Galloping through meadows, churning up earth.

Gaia, you are
More than fair,
To let us mortals share
A bit of your glory
A part of your story.
To let us hear
The music of this sphere.
To let us imagine that
Descended ancient star seeds
Became continents of feral trees.
To let us know of
Forestals in wild fruit homes
With dryads and elves who roam,
Caressing,
Blessing,
Touching,
Bird and beast fallen asleep
Far away in timbers deep.

All things are full of spirit, intention, a goal.
Attracted to that which is resonant with each soul.

Everything symbolic, full of meaning.
We live inside the planet's dreaming.

Gaia,
You make the most exotic dreams come true;
And more than that too,
You touch with such grace,
In every place,
With a hyper-dimensional view.
You can transform everything anew.

Dawn.
Stars on the dome of the night
At the edge of sight
Give way to sunrise in the mist.
An immense ball of flame—eclipse.

Gaia, your essence:
Babbles in the brooks of mountains,
Flows down through Nature's fountains,
Empties wide on the rivers of the plains,
Swirls in lakes forming sift-sand stains,
Rages mightily in tempestuous seas,
Blows through hollowed oak trees,
Morning sunbeams sparkle your gems,
Granting life to plant, leaf, stems.

And all this you entrust
To the part of you in all of us.
To the mystery you created within us.

Gaia, you have given birth to every living form.
Nurtured, raised, loved all that is born.
You have created the most intriguing art.
Somehow you have put the whole in every part.

The Greatest Love Story That's Ever Been Told

by Nick Good

In The Greatest Love Story That's Ever Been Told
The riches within us *together* unfold.
An adventure in eternity, with pause for rest
To arrive in a heaven we never had left.
Now, the Earth, a planet to save,
Soon the stars for the wild and brave.
The children of God, on a Love mission,
Hearts more powerful than nuclear fission.
A spirit exists in you and me
Same like the man who walked on the sea.
Together in purity, peace, and love
A doorway opens to a world above.
The potential of Human, ET, and God,
A child of Nature against all odds.
The wonder, the majesty, the power, the awe,
Reality soon like never before?
Be who you are and the journey starts
For the true, the kind, the pure of heart.
The children of God on a mission of love,
A message to deliver to the folks above:
The light that shines is for you and me
To be who we are, to be, to be.
Simple it sounds, not easy perhaps,
Sticky the web in which souls get trapped,
The game isn't real, it's all in the mind
Dive into your heart, the freedom to find.
Look to the stars, the heavens above,
Eyes closed or open but do it with love.
Nature's surprises forever are new,
The biggest one is *coming alive in you.*

The greatest love story that's ever been told—
Believe in that! Not the lies that've been sold.
The parasite now is losing its power,
Love dissolves fear in the final hour.
More than you dreamed and ever have known
Is coming from within you, by the love you have shown.
Peace is the key that opens the door,
Compassion the temple, courage the floor.
Now is the time to let your Self shine,
Forgiveness the path we walk this time.
Together we stand, the heavens await
One final act before it's too late:
Your love to show to one and all.
Compassion, will, cause—the war machines fall.
If a toxic world surrounds ourselves
'tis only a reflection of inner hells;
Change within to change the without,
Invoke who you are with a silent shout.
Now is the time, the final hour
In the eternal garden, 'tis time to flower.
The children of God on a mission in Love
Together, forever, through the stars above.

Copyright Nick Good 2007
Completed on Kauai, Hawaii

SUCCESS ULTRA NOW

BY DAVID WOLFE

A most amazing epoch we get to see.
What wondrous things we get to have, be.

Although removed, and over eons changed,
This race is not lost, nor completely estranged.
Somehow within
There is something new.
More majesty
Than our ancestors ever knew.

The hallowed halls of time
Speak a simple rhyme
All at once, and ever sober:
"It's not over until it's over."

Whether you're an elder or a youth
You can always step into a telephone booth,
Tear away your coat and hat
Emerge exactly where you're at.

Instead of being faster than a locomotive,
You can fast like a local native.

Instead of leaping tall buildings in a single bound,
You can stand tall, slender, proud.

Instead of fighting for truth, justice, and the American way,
You can live for youth, with zest, and the best ever day.

When you
Tear the glasses away
And see everything through an x-ray—
A focused beam.
Things are not what they seem.

There has been a distortion of light
Right in plain sight.

The Daily Planet has something to report:
"Its time for the last resort."

Success Ultra Now.

This is the age, the era born
To break the norm
And transform;
Recreate
Brutal human
Into divine ape
(Or an angel with a cape).

There is one last show:
From zero to superhero.
From Babylon to Avalon.

Like Clark Kent
Heaven sent.
From a distant sun
The archetype has come.

Our traditional test:
Lex Luthor: the evil nemesis,
Lois Lane: the damsel in distress,
Have only been a preparation
To deal with universal deception.
The legion of doom, greed,
Is well in the lead.
And the stakes are rising higher
The entire planet is on fire.
Now "saving the girl"
Means saving the world.

The grand cosmic drama
Is unfolding upon our Pachamama.
A better script, set, sound
Could not be found.
Planned, positioned, prepared from eons old,
This is the greatest love story ever told:
And it could go either way—
No one can say.

This is the moment we've all been waiting for.
And you are being called to become more
To step into your role
Whole
With all your soul.
In one last attempt before the end
To save the planet at the last second
By snatching victory out of the jaws of defeat
In a miraculous, harrowing feat.

How?

By envisioning a sacred "s"
For a start,
Right over your heart.

By imbibing health, strength, vitality,
While achieving with morality.

By enhancing laughter, loving, living,
By becoming more giving.

By mastering space, matter, power,
By opening like a flower.

By cultivating ease, grace, flow,
By learning to let go.

By receiving mythic clues,
From acting on spirit's cues.

By achieving wisdom, glory, might,
Through clever insight.

By cultivating bravery, charm,
To shield yourself from harm.

Remember:
Our powers may hide
But they're always somewhere inside.
The supersuit is underneath,
Something you yourself bequeath
By tearing away what isn't true
Revealing the real you
Brand new
Guided by virtue
With every motive, selection
Backed by intention.

Believe the hype,
The superhero archetype.
In order to save this spinning sphere
And arrive right here
And now.
We've got to evaporate lack
And get all our power back.

Think about the world today,
Utter transformation in every way.

All knowledge is now here.
What was far, has become near.

What was a mystery,
Has become clear.

Here we alight
On the brink of starflight.

Still on two feet
Finally discovering what to eat.

This is the moment:
We wash away the line
Separating human from divine.
And gain a true understanding
That we can escape a crash landing.

When you decide
That you are on for the ride
To the gods
It's a beacon, a sign,
That you're in it
For real this time.

A key step
Is out of debt
And servitude
And into the fortress of solitude.
And latitudes higher
Where you're going to rewire
And realize too:
You can be:
(Instantly)
A poet, shaman
Lover, magician,
Warrior, technician,
Alchemist, artist,
Yogi, psychonaut, spiritualist,
Hydrophile, herbalist,
Chi Gong Taoist,
A brave, brilliant, daring,
Respectful, caring.
Cheerful
Resourceful

Comical
Magical
Immortal
Who:
Lives in the imagination
Works all one's years in meditation
Plays the limitless
Game of consciousness
While inside is silent, in stillness.

In essence,
You can:
Live the best life ever
But you must be very clever!

Because you decide how high you fly.
You decide why.
You decide how much you'll try.
Don't be fooled:
You are in control of your soul.

All the deception, distortion, lies,
Are a blessing in disguise.

They help shatter the mold of the old.
And break our judgment hold.

Revealing:
That empathy, love, compassion,
Are back in fashion.

It's time to know the truth,
No matter how strange or uncouth.

It's time to take the oath
We will save the old growth.
And if we can't, we'll plant even more,
After all, we're the ones we've been waiting for.

It's time to face our greatest test
And our goal is complete success.
Within
It's the cosmic plan in flower
Right at this very hour.

Yes ......
You can be an angel
Or a super-ape.
Wear a suit
Over your cape.

When battling arch-villains
You can't be smokin' chillums;
Instead it's plant spirit medicine
Sacred mycelium
The cacti allies
Sacred jungle brews
And no more TV news.
Switch to another station
A meditation
On 144,000 ecstatic fans
High in the coliseum stands
Hovering above are your angels, guides,
Brought in from far and wide
Applauding, laughing for all they're worth
Because you've created paradise on Earth.
And once you've had this vision
You're on the mission.

The plot is hatched
Remain calm, detached.

Take one giant leap
By breathing in deep.

This is the hour of power.

Stay vigilant, aware,
Handle your affairs with care.

Keep yourself imbued
With Earth's superfoods.
Imbibe antidotes of light
Against kryptonite.
Recreate yourself anew,
Stripped of calcification too.

This is what you need to hear:
You're staying here
Whether you do or do not care
You can't escape to over there,
To an island, a mansion, even the moon
Anytime soon.
It is time to take a stand.
The environment is the issue at hand.
It's the only issue that's ever been.
And saving it is the only win.

To survive the hero's test,
You'll have to deflect bullets right off your chest.
But you don't need to see through lead.
Just be well read.
And fashion a plan
To do everything you can
To entice
Yourself into paradise.

So here are the instructions
Given by hand
Directly from galactic command:

To love
(everything you can think of).

To unlearn
(what you didn't earn).

To align
(for the first time).

To assist all
(while having a ball).

To dance
(in ecstatic trance).

To sing
(with birds, wind, everything).

To laugh
(with the riff-raff).

To x-ray envision
(success in your mission).

To dismantle: arcane ideology
(with free energy, folk technology).

To close the Hall of Justice
And open the Hall of Just Bliss.

The technology of Tao,
Success Ultra Now.

There never was a more holy age than ours.
This is the most spiritualized moment in history.
Onward we plunge
Into the oversoul, whole.

Where to begin, go?
By becoming a superhero
And playing your part
Through opening your heart.
And where to go after?

Into cosmic laughter.

This is the revolution,
This is the solution,
This is the truth in fusion.
Everything else is an illusion.

With this knowledge one soars faster
Escaping the eventide of disaster
Into the realm of the master
To live happily ever after.

Copyright David Wolfe 2006
Completed on Orcas Island, Washington

THE MYSTERY

BY NICK GOOD

From God, through Love, in Spirit and Soul,
Sleeping infinity, in eternity unfolds,
That I unbound receive the gift
With waters of Life have now been kissed.
To wander far, from the sweetest nest,
Immeasurable miles, yet never had left.
Thus the mystery, ever to solve:
What is this *Constancy* that does not evolve?
The stories spin, weaving the web,
The gods and angels dance with the dead.
The choices we make are not who we are,
Yet may lead us home from afar.
And through our pain, illusions crack,
What fear has stolen, love gives back.
Thus the mystery ever to solve:
What is this *Love* that does not evolve?
There we stand together in form
An Almighty canvas cannot long stay torn.
What appears to be, may not be so
As all is rent, this we know.
The Ocean breathes a mighty sigh,
Cosmic waves are surely nigh,
Are you ready for what must be?
The fruit must fall from the mighty tree.
Thus the mystery ever to solve:
What is this *Peace* that does not evolve?
We are what we are and forever are held
No matter the beliefs to which we weld;
There is a fire to melt this false bond,
Within your heart burns its sacred song,

What now seems solid, in chains of fear
Like candle wax will disappear.
Thus the mystery ever to solve:
What is this *Light* that does not evolve?
An eternal garden in which we play,
The children dream another day.
Forever the wonder together we spin
Until we let go, to that which we cling.
So off to the stars to spread the good news,
The perfect gift we never could lose.
Thus the mystery ever to solve:
What is this *Purity* that never evolves?
From pure love spirit unfolds,
The story of love now is told;
You and I, a dream come true,
What future will we sculpt anew?
This the gift, ever to cherish,
The Love we are never can perish.
Thus the mystery ever to solve:
What is this *Compassion* that does not evolve?
And so the mystery through us revealed
The seeds of God, across the cosmic field.
To feel Love in unconscious mobs
Express Itself, against all odds.
The world is poised, are you ready to see?
To know what you are, what you always will be?
Thus the mystery ever to solve:
What is this *Wonder* that does not evolve?

Appendix A: Ormus

Ormus Properties

David Radius Hudson made a number of discoveries concerning the properties of "strange matter" related to the platinum-group metals that he chemically released from Arizonan basalt rock. This strange matter has subsequently been termed *Ormus*.

Hudson determined that metals, when they are infolded back into their Ormus form, lose 4/9ths of their mass. When these Ormus elements are converted back to the metallic state, they regain 4/9ths of their mass. This indicates that the mass was somehow slipped into another dimension and then brought back. Hudson theoretically proved that the atomic nuclei of Ormus elements are deformed into egg, banana, or bottle shapes instead of near-spheres, thereby deforming space-time even more intensely than normal atomic nuclei and opening up a larger rift in the fabric of matter. They are drawing in large quanta of free energy from the aether. David Hudson has claimed room-temperature superconductivity of the Ormus elements. He identified fuel cell applications for such elements. According to Barry Carter (who is currently the Internet's leading authority on Ormus), an Ormus osmium battery the size of a car battery can be charged to power a vehicle for 2000 miles (3220 kilometers). Ordinary electric cars use twenty normal batteries to do the same thing. In a computer, an Ormus osmium battery could store enough power that you would only need to charge it once a year. Hudson also appears to have identified that Ormus elements can completely shield energy and radiation except at their resonant frequencies; this insight alone can have shocking implications for all aerospace technologies such as coating spacecraft with Ormus elements to shield them from space radiation—alien spacecraft are said to be coated with such materials. Ormus elements in and on those ships may give them properties of living machines. Remember, Ormus is atomic matter that is, by all estimations, conscious.

In his research, Barry Carter has noted that Ormus appears to be capable of the following phenomena:

❖ Meissner field activity (an electromagnetic field without polarity that can cause spontaneous levitation when it is moved over the Earth's magnetic field)

❖ Tachyon events (faster-than-light phenomena)

❖ Josephson tunneling (Ormus minerals have been noted to jump or teleport from one place to another)

❖ Superfluid behavior (this causes energy to flow without friction in our dimension, and may open the way to scientifically understanding ghosts and apparitions)

❖ Bose-Einstein condensates (a group of atoms in phase and therefore behaving as one atom—this type of quantum coherence could scientifically explain how clairvoyance or telepathy occur)

❖ Homeopathic properties of water (Ormus elements may be responsible for the power of succussed or super-diluted herbal medicines).

Alchemy

The insights of Ormus physics, nuclear physics, and quantum physics continue to point to the stunning realization that the great alchemists of history were onto something major. Today we are taught that ancient alchemists were juvenile chemists who did not know what they were doing, and that all alchemy is either useless arcane chemistry or a mere metaphor for the enlightenment process. Yet there are those among us who never bought these ideas. Those of you who can read between the lines of the surviving works of the great alchemists understand that there is actually a physical science of alchemy. The great alchemists are talking about an advanced form of chemistry and quantum physics, not just spiritual metaphors. The alchemists knew something that they deliberately obscured so that the secrets could not be penetrated without the proper intent.

Although not critical for most non-scientific laypeople in the overall discussion of Ormus (but critical for scientific Ormus researchers), there is a possibility that the class of elements we currently call Ormus may have three (or more) sub-classes within it, referred to by traditional alchemists as the salt, sulfur, and mercury of the metal. So, for example, Ormus copper (we believe) refers to the "salt of the metal copper" in traditional alchemy because the ancient alchemists would have created Ormus copper out of copper by the projection of copper onto molten salt. There may be in addition two other forms of Ormus copper, namely: the sulfur and mercury of copper. The words "salt," sulfur," and "mercury" as used by alchemists in this context are code words and have nothing to do with the molecules of salt, sulfur, and mercury as we know them in modern science. As a side note, it is possible that the mercury of the different metals is all the same.

WHERE IS ORMUS FOUND?

Ormus is unusually concentrated in many natural materials and places. Ormus elements are prevalent in our immediate environment.

What we consider dirt (oxygen, carbon, silicon, aluminum, iron, calcium, etc.) is often more than just these simple elements—Ormus elements are also present.

Higher-altitude valleys (the Himalaya, the Andes) are richer in aetherialized Ormus substances in the atmosphere than are lower-altitude regions. This was also observed by Wilhelm Reich, who noted that higher-altitude regions are richer in Orgone energy—which was his term for the superconductive flow of energy between aetherialized Ormus compounds in the atmosphere.

Volcanic regions, especially Hawaii and Central America, are known to be rich in Ormus. Occasionally a lava rock will have unusually high concentrations of Ormus. Intuitive Hawaiians call such a rock a *pohaku*—a stone with consciousness.

The Hawaiians have a saying: *'O ke alealea leu o Mana'* or 'the salt-pond of mana.' This denotes their understanding that salts and salt ponds can contain high concentrations of Ormus elements. We have extracted Ormus from Celtic sea salt, Himalayan pink salt, and the salt found at Eden Hot Springs. The highest natural concentration of Ormus elements is found at the Dead Sea and in Dead Sea salts. The focus of alchemists on salt is not accidental.

Fresh, cold, mountain spring water is also known to be rich in Ormus, at least for the first hundred meters out of the ground.

In general, flower pollen and nectar, chitin (animal and insect exoskeletons), and mushroom spores are considered highly concentrated sources of Ormus.

OTHER PLACES ORMUS ELEMENTS ARE FOUND

The Internet Ormus community (Barry Carter, *et al.*) has theorized that Ormus minerals are perhaps thousands of times more common than their associated metals. Research by Hudson, Carter, and many garage alchemists indicates that Ormus elements are more stable than metals. There is more of it present in the world. It is relatively easy to alchemically process metal atoms and turn them into Ormus atoms; it is difficult to do the reverse. This type of evidence suggests reasonable stability in the Ormus state.

Ormus likes to get into fractures of rock (especially fissures in mica and quartz). It appears that Ormus sometimes likes tight, quiet places, probably so it does not have to move in relation to magnetic fields. Ormus has been known to spontaneously jump away from strong electromagnetic fields. The Vortrap device blueprinted by Barry Carter uses this and other characteristics of the Ormus elements to trap and concentrate Ormus elements in water.

Ormus has been found in charcoal briquettes as well as hydrocarbons of various sorts (plant oils, motor oil, gasoline, rolls of plastic sheeting, plastic tubes, etc.).

STEALTH ATOMS

Ormus elements can also be understood as strange forms of carbon because they can mimic certain behaviors of carbon or appear to be carbon when a spectroscope is used for mineral analysis. We believe that Viktor Schauberger used the word *kohle-stoffe* (a higher aspect of carbon) in order to signify Ormus. In the English-language versions of Viktor Schauberger's work, *Living Energies* and the Eco-Technology series, author Callum Coats translated the German word *kohle-stoffe* to *carbone* to denote the difference between standard carbon and levitative forms of carbon (*carbone* or Ormus).

The following relationships were noted by David Hudson:

Ormus rhodium often appears to be carbon. This is extremely interesting because rhodium as a metal is a massive atom in size, whereas carbon is relatively small by comparison. Ormus rhodium is likely the same size as carbon and, like carbon, appears black to light.

Ormus rhodium dioxide appears to be iron oxide and analyzes as iron and oxygen.

Hydrogen-reduced Ormus rhodium will analyze as silicon and aluminum.

Annealed hydrogen-reduced Ormus rhodium analyzes as silica and calcium.

This "mimicking" of other elements is probably related to the size of the Ormus elements. They are smaller than their completely unfolded metallic states. David Hudson reported that Ormus rhodium would appear to be other elements depending on the state of his Ormus purification process.

More Interesting Insights into Ormus

In our own research lab we uncovered a point of interest: you can move a metal towards its Ormus state by doing your best to remove all energy from the metal while disassociating the metal into very small atomic clusters. With gold this cluster size is no cluster at all; it must be one atom in size.) Interestingly, this is the exact opposite of what is normally done in chemistry (adding energy to create chemical reactions).

During a water-heat extraction process, heat-resistant mineral skeletons (probably Ormus elements) drop out of mammalian cartilage, liver tissue, or other organ tissue and into solution in the water. These skeletons appear to contain the codes necessary for the accelerated reconstruction of cartilage or liver tissue or other organ tissue if the skeletons are ingested by other similar mammals. This appears to be what Dr. Royal Lee discovered and is likely the basis of his special line of nutritional supplements called Standard Process.

Ormus, Human Levitation, and Flight

Ormus elements are associated with levitation (displacing the force of gravity). The theory states that if one is saturated in enough Ormus, then levitation or flight become possible.

We grew up enchanted by the old kung fu movies where the heroes and villains could fly through the trees with extraordinary abilities. Modern-day epics like *Crouching Tiger, Hidden Dragon* and *Hero* are a testimony to an age gone by. Is this all fantasy, or do myth and reality interface somewhere? Something deep inside us instinctively knows that they do. We may have caged a wild natural aspect of our powers within a prison of ordinariness, mind-numbing taxation, and status quo. Supernatural heroics awaken a sleeping part of ourselves.

So what did help those kung fu guys fly? The evidence is pointing to several key factors: training, awareness, attitude (knowing), as well as a particular type of wild red asparagus consumed in a regimen with mushroom spring water teas and goji berries.

Appendix B: A Summary of the Seven Principles of Huna

The Huna teachings are similar to the Egyptian teachings of initiation into the Order of Melchizedek during the Third Dynasty. *Huna,* in Hawaiian, means "secret." Huna, in its purest form, is ancient knowledge enabling individuals to connect to their highest aspirations, wisdom, skills, and abilities. Understanding and utilizing the seven principles of Huna enables each individual to connect directly with the powers of healing and harmony through the outreach of universal consciousness. This healing art and earth science is spiritual in nature, and experiencing its concepts gives us the opportunity to integrate mind, body, and spirit. One might acknowledge the Huna teachings as a series of nature's tools that help with the development of inner knowledge and enhanced innate psychic abilities.

The Seven Principles of Huna

IKE—We Make our Reality.

MAKIA—Energy Flows where Attention Goes.

MANA—All Power Comes from Within.

MANAWA—Now is the Moment of Power.

KALA—All Change is Possible.

PONO—Harmony/Effectiveness is a Measure of Truth.

ALOHA—To Love is to Share the Happiness of the Breath of Life With.

APPENDIX C: THE PRAYER OF BOUNTY

Lord, Please Open My Mind, Heart, and Being to Your Complete Limitless Bountiful Prosperity and Love.

Please Help All Things That I Think, Say, and Do Be Filled with Your Complete Limitless Bountiful Prosperity and Love.

Please Allow Me to Be Blessed with the Riches and Bounty of Your Heavens and Your Earth Always.

Please Lead Me, Guide Me, and Direct Me into Your Life, into Your Light, into Your Love, and into Your Complete Limitless, Bountiful Prosperity and Love. Celebrating Life as It Is from You Lord Now and Forever.

Thank You Lord, Thank You Lord, Thank You Lord, Thank You Lord, Thank You Lord, Thank You Lord, Thank You Lord, Thank YOU.

www.howardwills.com

REFERENCES

1. For the rest of his life, **Captain John Newton** observed the anniversary of **May 10, 1748,** as the day of his conversion, a day of humiliation in which he subjected his will to a higher power. The first known publication of the hymn was 1779.

2. **Steven M. Greer,** MD, is the founder of The Disclosure Project, a nonprofit research effort to fully disclose the facts about UFOs, extraterrestrial intelligence, and classified advanced energy and propulsion systems. More than four hundred government, military, and intelligence community witnesses have testified to their direct, personal, first-hand experience with UFOs, ETs, ET technology, and the cover-up that keeps this information secret.

   In this book: *Hidden Truth—Forbidden Knowledge,* Dr. Greer provides his own personal disclosure based on years of high-level meetings with more than four hundred and fifty military and government-connected insiders and whistle-blowers, as well as briefings with senior government officials, such as former CIA Director R. James Woolsey, members of the US Senate, and senior UN officials.

   In addition to these disclosures, *Hidden Truth—Forbidden Knowledge* unveils the actual contact experiences Dr. Greer has had with UFOs and extraterrestrial civilizations, beginning as a child. In one of the most amazing and moving personal stories ever shared, he explains how after a prolonged near-death experience at age seventeen, he entered a state of cosmic consciousness and found that he could psychically communicate with extraterrestrial intelligences. Later this led to numerous Close Encounters of the 5th Kind: contact with ETs initiated by Dr. Greer and later by larger groups of people through CSETI (Center for the Study of Extraterrestrial Intelligence).

   About The Disclosure Project Dr. Greer has stated:

   > Beginning in 1993, I started an effort that was designed to identify firsthand military and government witnesses to UFO events and projects, as well as other evidence to be used in a public disclosure. From 1993, we spent considerable time and resources briefing the Clinton Administration, including CIA Director

James Woolsey, senior military officials at the Pentagon, and select members of Congress, among others. In April of 1997, more than a dozen such government and military witnesses were assembled in Washington, DC, for briefings with Congressmen, Pentagon officials and others. There, we specifically requested open Congressional Hearings on the subject. None were forthcoming.

In 1998, we set out to "privatize" the disclosure process by raising the funds to videotape, edit, and organize over 100 military and government witnesses to UFO events and projects. We had estimated that between $2 million and $4 million would be needed to do this on a worldwide basis. By August of 2000 only about 5% of this amount had been raised, but we decided to proceed since further delay was deemed imprudent given the serious issues involved here. So beginning in August we began creating the Witness Archive Project and we set about the task of traveling all over the world to interview these witnesses in broadcast-quality digital video format. Due to the severe limitation of funds, this effort was predominantly prepared by myself and a few other volunteers roughly from August 2000 through December 2000.

For more information about Dr. Steven Greer and The Disclosure Project please visit: www.disclosureproject.org

3. Photograph taken May 23, 2006, by the *Cassini-Huygens* probe on its Mission to Saturn and Titan. Please review the following links:
   http://saturn.jpl.nasa.gov/multimedia/images/raw/casJPGFull
   S02/N00007211.jpg
   http://saturn.jpl.nasa.gov/multimedia/images/raw/casJPGFull
   S02/N00007442.jpg
   http://saturn.jpl.nasa.gov/multimedia/images/raw/casJPGFull
   S02/N00007453.jpg
   http://saturn.jpl.nasa.gov/multimedia/images/raw/casJPGBrowse
   S02/N00007448.jpg
   http://saturn.jpl.nasa.gov/multimedia/images/raw/casJPGBrowse
   S02/N00007450.jpg

http://saturn.jpl.nasa.gov/multimedia/images/raw/casJPGBrowse
    S02/N00007451.jpg

http://saturn.jpl.nasa.gov/multimedia/images/raw/casJPGBrowse
    S02/N00007488.jpg

4. **The Canadian Shield**—also called the Precambrian Shield, Laurentian Shield, Bouclier Canadien (French), or Laurentian Plateau—is a large thin-soiled area over a part of the North American craton (a deep, common, joined bedrock region) in eastern and central Canada and adjacent portions of the United States, composed of base rock dating to the Precambrian Era (between 4.5 billion and 540 million years ago). The Canadian Shield is almost circular, which gives it an appearance of a warrior's shield or a giant horseshoe. It is a subsection of the Laurentia craton signifying the area of greatest glacial impact (scraping down to bare rock), resulting in the thin soils we see there today.

5. **Midi-chlorians** (also spelled "midi-clorians" or "midichlorians") are mysterious organisms in the fictional *Star Wars* universe, first mentioned in the prequel trilogy. They are said to be microscopic life-forms that reside within the cells of all living things and communicate with the Force. Midi-chlorians comprise a collective consciousness and intelligence, forming links between everything living and The Force. They are symbionts with all other living things; that is, without them, life could not exist. The Jedi have learned how to listen to and coordinate the midi-chlorians. If they quiet their minds, they can hear the midi-chlorians speaking to them, telling them the will of The Force. In order to be a Jedi or a Sith, one must have a high concentration of midi-chlorians in one's cells. This idea is very similar to the concept of MANA and Ormus, as well as to the seventeenth-century philosopher Gottfried Leibniz's theory of monads—infinitesimal elementary particles that exist as amalgams of matter and consciousness.

    The word "midi-chlorian" appears to be a blend of "mitochondrion" and "chloroplast," two organelles found in real cells and thought to have evolved from bacteria as endosymbionts inside other cells, as purported in the endosymbiotic theory. *Star Wars* creator George Lucas has indeed stated that the midi-chlorians are based on the endosymbiotic theory, and it appears that in the story of Anakin Skywalker, Lucas wanted to create a more modern "virgin birth" in the *Star Wars* saga that was as much based on science as on philosophy and religion, with the mythic "givers of life" being microscopic life-forms rather than gods.

6. In the *Star Wars* universe, **the Jedi mind trick** is a Force power. Jedi who know the power can, by using The Force, influence the actions of other "less conscious" sentient beings.

   Some residents of the *Star Wars* galaxy are able to resist the technique, namely the Hutts and Toydarians. The precise reasons are unknown but could be attributed to their having different thought patterns from the humans who are performing it. Especially strong-willed individuals are also able to resist the trick. Anakin Skywalker confirms this in a conversation with Padmé Amidala during *Star Wars Episode II: Attack of the Clones,* after she jokingly asks him if he will use the trick on her. Droids also resist mind tricks, because mind tricks can only be used on something with a mind, which excludes droids.

   The Jedi mind trick has been compared to similar real-world tricks performed using "mentalism." This is a broad term for creating illusions in the mind of another, a feat performed many times by the famous British mentalist Derren Brown.

7. **Viktor Schauberger** is considered the father of Living Water. A famous naturalist from Austria who discovered how water becomes enlivened in the environment through implosion, he was the first scientist to clearly point out that water gains the quality of life and ennoblement based on double-spiral vortex spin implosion motion. Initially, Schauberger developed many methods of tapping into the power of water to support local industry, such as the movement of logs in a stream or artificially constructed water pathways. He considered water to be a living being that could make intelligent choices of where to flow based on changing conditions in the atmosphere and land. He observed that water could literally levitate, defy Newtonian Laws of Physics, and emerge in high mountain springs. As his career progressed he built free-energy, turbine-type machines based on the

implosion principles of vortex spin. Schauberger pointed out that most modern technology is based on expending and wasting energy through explosion, which increases entropy and pollution, whereas energy could be produced through implosion, which increases ectropy or creative forces without any pollution. His technological insights are critical to developing a pollution-free planet.

Recommended Viktor Schauberger reading (as translated by Callum Coats and published by Gateway Books in the United Kingdom):
Living Energies
The Water Wizard
The Fertile Earth
Nature As Teacher
Energy Evolution

8. The widely used Quechua name **ayahuasca** (pronounced eye-a-waska) has two interrelated yet distinct meanings and referents: 1) a giant vine named *Banisteriopsis caapi* that grows in the Amazon rainforest and contains various psychoactive harmala alkaloids, 2) pharmacologically complex psychoactive infusions prepared from the vine for shamanic, folk-medicinal, and religious purposes. Sections of vine are macerated and boiled alone or with leaves from any of a large number of other plants, including *Psychotria viridis* (*chakruna* in Quechua) or *Diplopterys cabrerana* (also known as *chacropanga*). The resulting brew contains MAO-inhibiting harmala alkaloids and the powerful hallucinogenic alkaloid N,N-dimethyltryptamine (DMT), a psychedelic that is active orally only when combined with MAO-inhibiting (MAOI) compounds. Harmala alkaloids in *Banisteriopsis caapi* serve as MAOIs in ayahuasca. Western brews sometimes substitute plant sources such as Syrian Rue or other harmala-containing plants in lieu of the *Banisteriopsis caapi* vine, but the vine itself is always central to traditional usage.

9. "Several years ago, my friend Dr. Bernard Jensen came to visit me while I was in Tucson. We spent four hours talking about health and the mind. He told me the following story that I think the world should hear. 'Many years ago, when I was still a young man, there were rumors that the Virgin Mary had been appearing at Fatima, and that many

people were being healed. I wanted to see if this was true, so I went there. While I was there, there was also another doctor visiting, a very famous doctor, one who had won a Nobel Prize. Dr. Alexis Carrell had received the Nobel Prize for proving that the cell, when properly nourished and cleansed, was essentially immortal. He was conducting a study to try and determine why some people were being healed and others were not. For there had been thousands of people who traveled there for healings. Some people couldn't walk, some were blind, others had incurable diseases. Only a small percentage received healings, and those healings were considerable, far beyond anything that science could explain.

"Dr. Carrell had designed a questionnaire that had more than a hundred questions. He gave this questionnaire to everyone who received a healing; and apparently there were hundreds. There was one question that everyone answered with the same response. That question was: What were you thinking when you received the healing? Now get this, for this is important. Thousands of people asked for a healing, only a small percentage got a healing. Everyone who got a healing answered this one question with the exact same answer. 'What were you thinking when you received the healing?' The answer was 'I was praying for someone else to be healed.'"

From the book *Cleanse And Purify Thyself, Book 2* by Richard Anderson, pp. 206–207.

10. The Howard Wills *Prayers and Affirmations* © 2005, All Rights Reserved. These prayers and affirmations are for humanity. Please feel free to send them electronically through email, copy them, and distribute them for your personal use. If you are interested in publishing any or all of these prayers and affirmations or translating them into another language, please contact www.howardwills.com.

11. *Been Down So Long* by The Doors © Doors Music Company ASCAP. Well I've been down so god damn long that it looks like up to me. Well I've been down so very damn long that it looks like up to me. Why don't one of you people come on and set me free?

RESOURCES

THE FRUIT TREE PLANTING FOUNDATION

www.fruittreefoundation.org

"Nothing in the world gives me more satisfaction than planting fruit trees. As I have always chosen to channel my energy and finances into environmentally friendly, sustainable and healthy directions, I founded the non-profit Fruit Tree Planting Foundation as a place where we could all vote with our money for a better, happier, more abundant, forested future on Earth. Please read about our foundation and decide that you want to donate your time, energy and/or money to this worthy cause."

—DAVID WOLFE, JD

The Fruit Tree Planting Foundation (FTPF) is a unique nonprofit charity dedicated to planting edible, fruitful trees and plants to benefit needy populations and improve the surrounding air, soil, and water.

Our programs strategically plant orchards where the harvest will best serve the community for decades to follow, at places such as homeless shelters, drug rehab centers, low-income areas, international hunger relief sites, and animal sanctuaries. FTPF's projects benefit the environment, human health, and animal welfare—all at once!

FTPF's goal is straightforward: to collectively plant eighteen billion fruit trees for a healthy planet (approximately three for every person alive). Fruit trees heal the environment by cleaning the air, improving soil quality, preventing erosion, creating animal habitat, sustaining valuable water sources, and providing healthy nutrition.

We envision a place where one can have a summer picnic under the shade of a fruit tree, breathe the clean air it generates, listen to the songbirds it attracts, and not have to bring anything other than an appetite for the healthy fruits growing overhead. A world where one can take a walk in the park during a lunch break, pick and eat a variety of delicious fruits, plant the seeds so others can eventually do the same, and provide an alternative to buying environmentally destructive, illness-causing, chemically laden products.

FTPF has planted thousands of fruit trees all over the world and provided advice and training for others to do so as well. We have launched a series of exciting new programs and we need your help!

Your tax-deductible charitable investment will help us realize our dream of a sustainable planet for generations to come. As you find you are interested in donating, please send a check or money order payable to:

The Fruit Tree Planting Foundation   www.ftpf.org
P.O. Box 900113   info@ftpf.orgSan Diego, CA
92190   Phone: 831-621-8096
USA   Toll-free: 877-884-7570
Fax: 831-621-7978

While we will be sending you a receipt for your donation, you may want to make a note of this transaction for tax purposes. Thanks for taking action on this important issue.

Success Ultra Now

Amazing Grace contains a clarion call for those of us who can hear it. Now is the time to rise against seemingly overwhelming odds, and play our superhero parts upon the great stage of life in the greatest love story that has ever been told.

Success Ultra Now *(SUN)* is the comprehensive holistic support strategy that enables us to answer this call.

We welcome you to Success Ultra Now. We welcome you to the experience of accepting the mission of fulfilling your highest destiny. Success Ultra Now offers practical experiential-based programs that provide you with the specific tools and strategies to answer the call of your soul and discover the inherent magic within the universe. Success Ultra Now is an inclusive companion program for ensuring the highest successes referred to in this book.

Program components include:

SUNPOP Guided Inner Journey CD

This audio recording takes us on a guided visualization meditation. The inner journey helps to re-establish a natural flow of pure unlimited thought potential as it pours into the physical realm by removing energetic distortions. This is a must-do program for the superhero.

The Best Day Ever Affirmation Art Print

This daily affirmation superimposed upon a beautiful sunrise on a high-quality art print is designed to be used in harmony with the *SUNPOP* guided inner journey.

Gentle Warrior—Adventure Retreat in Kauai, Hawaii

This is an initiatory adventure training offered only to those individuals who have read *Amazing Grace,* practiced the *SUNPOP* guided inner journey, attended a David Wolfe retreat, passed a special interview, and who are ready at the solar, soul, and cellular level. The Gentle Warrior Program is for those who wish to 100% embody and discover the teachings contained in this book. The program is an intense journey of self-discovery including superfood nutritional strategies, meditation, Chi Gong, Vision Quest, alignment with seven elements, seven principles of Huna, swimming with dolphins, story telling, *SUNPOP* inner journey, personal coaching from Gentle Warrior facilitators, and much more. Three-, Seven-, fourteen-, and forty-two-day formats available by special arrangement.

www.successultranow.com

THE BEST DAY EVER

David Wolfe's Peak Performance Archives are available at this dynamic website:

www.thebestdayever.com

(Warning! The contents of this website may cause you to have The Best Day Ever!)

A Special Message from David Wolfe

I have so many tapes of my past lectures, so many notes I have taken over the years, so many great health and success secrets, so many incredible bits of information that my office and I are overloaded. I literally spent a couple years wondering what to do with all this great stuff! Should I put it into more books? More DVDs? More audio recordings? This stuff is not doing the planet any good sitting here in my office! Then I met a man who recommended that we start a subscription website. We did! We took my material and combined it with information and seminars by the leading women and men in the nutrition and peak performance field. Now all this material is online at thebestdayever.com and I am so excited!

On this one website you will have access to a literally priceless amount of the most valuable, peak-performance nutritional seminars, documents, interviews, product reviews, and videos ever assembled in one place at one time!

The detailed information found on the website www.thebestday ever.com demonstrates how to:

❖ Shed those stubborn, unwanted pounds.
❖ Experience up-to-date information from America's foremost raw lifestyle authorities (both women and men).
❖ Leap ahead of the curve in the health and peak performance field.
❖ Achieve an extraordinary level of energy.
❖ Radically rejuvenate yourself physically, emotionally, and spiritually.
❖ Achieve a remarkable level of sensuality, charisma, and sex appeal.
❖ Enjoy every second of life and really experience The Best Day Ever!
❖ Explode your creativity.
❖ Sleep two to four fewer hours each night and wake up feeling better than ever!
❖ Add years (if not decades) to your lifespan.
❖ Take immediate advantage of secret, yet crucial diet information.

This incredible website gives you complete ACCESS to my text, audio, and video library containing dozens of lectures and CONFIDENTIAL files on nutrition, health, minerals, rejuvenation programs, and exotic information, including on how to heal some of the most stubborn conditions known to humanity.

Also, the website includes professional nutrition coaching forums where you can get up-to-the-moment answers to your questions. You will also hear live interviews with me on a monthly basis, where I answer your questions and bring you up to date on the latest and greatest. Also, if you are interested, you can tap into my monthly diary blog.

I am a BIG believer in saturating oneself with positive, empowering information. Our website, www.thebestdayever.com, has been designed to literally bombard you with inspirational text, audio, and video. Much of the material on the site you can download directly onto your computer or iPod and use whenever you want!

www.thebestdayever.com is essentially my uncensored online magazine that allows you to instantly access the latest, most fascinating information in the field. No more waiting by the mailbox. All I do, all day every day, is pursue and live the cutting edge of health, beauty, nutrition, peak performance, vegetarian diets, and especially superfood diets. This information allows you to leap miles ahead of the curve and create astounding rejuvenation and healing now without having to make the same mistakes that tens of thousands of others have made.

Why am I doing this? Because the information that is in my brain and computer is expanding far faster than I can publish it in books. I have been perplexed as to what to do with it all. Eventually, the answer appeared: create an online magazine for you! This site was created to give you immediate access to leading-edge information that can help you instantly enhance the quality of your life.

This is the first time in the history of my career as a peak-performance consultant that I've packaged together so many compelling, life-changing programs into one jam-packed website. Nothing like this website is available on the Internet. This is truly a one-of-a-kind phenomenon. The future is now!

www.thebestdayever.com is constantly updated. This is an ever-growing resource for you and your whole family to enjoy.

If you are inspired to achieve an exceptional state of health, success, beauty, fitness, awareness, joy, sensuality, accomplishment, peak performance, and (most important), fun, then these Peak–Performance Archives are for you!

Check it out and HAVE THE BEST DAY EVER!!!
www.thebestdayever.com

THE BIAVIIAN MOTHERSHIP
How to Order Your Ticket Aboard the Biaviian Mothership

Our friend Riley Martin was downloaded 144,000 "ticket" symbols for humanity during his stay on the Great Mothership in 1975. It is his duty as a human ambassador for the Biaviians to create an individual ticket (from the 144,000 designs) for anyone who requests it. To have Riley make a ticket for you, please visit his website www.rileymartin.tv and follow instructions on how to get your very own "symbol."

RECOMMENDED SUPERHERO RESOURCES

Available from **www.davidwolfe.com**

Organic Superfoods and Superherbs

Sacred Chocolate (simply the best chocolate brand ever—real superhero chocolate)
Sun Is Shining (a combination of raw, powdered superfoods)
Cacao Beans (raw chocolate)
Cacao Nibs (raw chocolate pieces)
Cacao Powder
Cacao Butter
Goji Berries
Goji Berry Powder
Maca
Maca Extract Extreme
Acai
Hempseeds
Hemp Protein
Wild Honey
Bee Pollen
Spirulina
Blue-Green Algae
Chlorella
Marine Phytoplankton

Kelp Powder
Medicinal Mushroom Extracts
(Reishi, Cordyceps, Maitake, Shiitake, Lion's Mane, Chaga, etc.)
Camu Berry Powder
Nutmeg (whole)
Schizandra Berries
Noni Leaf
Pau D'Arco Bark
Cat's Claw Bark
Chuchuhuasi Bark
Sacha Jergon Root

Superhero Supplements (www.davidwolfe.com)

Beauty Enzymes
Blue Mangosteen (antioxidant)
MSM (methyl-sulfonyl-methane)
Activated Liquid Zeolites (Natural Cellular Defense)
Celtic Grey Mineral Sea Salt
MegaHydrate (created by Dr. Patrick Flanagan)
Crystal Energy (created by Dr. Patrick Flanagan)
Ormus Gold (created and produced by David Wolfe and his science team)

Superhero Accessories

EMF necklace shields (Patrick Flanagan's Sensor I, II, or III, Q-link, etc.)
Quartz crystals (programmable by consciousness) ... (widely available in nature and at gem shops and shows)
A Biaviian symbol (Riley Martin at www.rileymartin.tv)
A Zapper (see www.thebestdayever.com)

OTHER PROJECTS BY DAVID WOLFE

Books

The Sunfood Diet Success System
Sunfood Living (Companion to The Sunfood Diet)
Eating For Beauty
Naked Chocolate
Superfoods: The Food and Medicine of the Future

Compact Disc Audio Programs

David Wolfe's 21-Day Weight Loss and Peak Performance Program
(www.21daystohealth.com)

Compact Disc Music

This Cooked Planet by The Healing Waters Band
Ten original songs
All Is One by The Healing Waters Band
Twelve original songs
(David Wolfe is the drummer and executive producer)

Book, Video, and DVD Sets

The LongevityNOW Program

David Wolfe Websites

www.davidwolfe.com
www.thebestdayever.com
www.sacredchocolate.com
www.ftpf.org

Other Books by Nick Good

Soul Consciousness: The Love Story
The Biology of Peace: Cancer, the Natural Answer

Other Projects by Nick Good

Success Ultra Now Human Potential Products and Services
Gentle Warrior Training Retreats
Success Posters
SUN Personal Optimization Program

Nick Good Websites

www.successultranow.com

Until further notice, celebrate everything.